# Rejoice and Be Glad

*Daily Reflections for Easter to Pentecost 2022*

Susan H. Swetnam

D1329728

**LITURGICAL PRESS**

Collegeville, Minnesota

www.litpress.org

*Nihil Obstat:* Rev. Robert Harren, J.C.L., *Censor Deputatus.*
*Imprimatur:* ✠ Most Rev. Donald J. Kettler, J.C.L., D.D., Bishop of St. Cloud, July 1, 2021.

Cover design by Monica Bokinskie. Cover art courtesy of Getty Images.

ISSN: 2578-7004 (Print)
ISSN: 2578-7012 (Online)

ISBN: 978-0-8146-6650-0          978-0-8146-6611-1 (e-book)

# Introduction

When Easter joy bursts upon us, we might well think of this great feast as a triumphant conclusion. Lenten penances are over, and somber liturgy is replaced by joyful celebration as the Gloria once again sounds and the light of Easter Vigil candles is passed from person to person. The Easter liturgy speaks gloriously of fulfillment, proclaiming that Christ's suffering is past and his sacrifice as the Lamb of God redeems our sins. Our ancient enemy, death, has been banished.

Even the created world (at least for those of us in the northern hemisphere) testifies that "Lo, the winter is past!" (cf. Song 2:11). Fourth-century Byzantine church father St. John Chrysostom acknowledged this harmony of theology and the natural world in an Easter homily, connecting the resurrection and the new "roses, violets, and other flowers" as mutually reinforcing signs of God's ever-renewing love.

Yet the readings for the Easter season demonstrate that instead of inviting Jesus' followers to relax into a sense of completion, the original Easter Sunday confronted them with a serious *"What now?"* moment. The resurrection shook pre-existing assumptions and comfortable paradigms, so it's no wonder that Jesus' followers initially responded with doubt and fear, confusion and debate. How could this be true? What did it mean? How were they to live their lives now? With whom were they supposed to share this good news?

More than two thousand years later, we have the wisdom of theologians, mystics, saints, and teachers to inform our faith. But all who seek to live the Easter mystery today will find those still evocative questions. Christ still asks, "[W]ho do you say that I am?" (Mark 8:29), and we still entreat, "[W]hat are we to do . . . ?" (Acts 2:37). Fears, doubts, and trials haven't disappeared—indeed, our world offers new challenges as resonant as those the apostles faced.

The Easter readings take us right into the heart of the ever-evolving process of becoming true disciples. Their narrative covers about thirty years, beginning with the resurrection, through the forty days when Jesus appeared to the apostles, to his ascension and the descent of the Holy Spirit at Pentecost, through the earliest persecutions and martyrdoms, to Paul's conversion and missionary journeys, and ending with Paul's house arrest in Rome around 60 CE. That's a lot of church history to grasp in just a few weeks!

Yet the sheer drama of these events and the perennial relevance of the readings' themes draw us in, inviting us to claim kinship with Peter, Stephen, Paul, and others as we marvel at their incredible fortitude. As we walk this venerable path in our imaginations each spring, we're encouraged to grow a little wiser every year, to consider ever-more-deeply the key questions about calling, about forgiveness and grace, about the balance of surrender and initiative, about community with one another and relationship with the divine, about persistence and courage.

I hope these reflections will enhance this year's Easter journey for you, helping you use this precious season as a time not just for rejoicing but also for exploration, opening, and renewed commitment to your own apostolic calling.

# Reflections

## Radical Reframing

**Readings:** Acts 10:34a, 37-43; Col 3:1-4 or 1 Cor 5:6b-8; John 20:1-9 or Luke 24:1-12

**Scripture:**
For they did not yet understand the Scripture that he had to rise from the dead. (John 20:9)

**Reflection:** And so it begins, this season when we are encouraged to "rejoice and be glad" (Ps 118:24), marveling at God's grace, glorying in a new covenant.

Several years ago a woman who had fully absorbed that spirit congratulated us musicians after the Easter Vigil. "How beautiful!" she exclaimed. "And fitting. Can you imagine the joy that first Easter morning, when they found the empty tomb? I wish I'd been there to celebrate!"

Well, not exactly. That night the woman's enthusiasm had overrun her attentiveness to the exact words of the Easter Gospel, which chronicle Jesus' followers' initial astonishment and lack of comprehension.

With the benefit of hindsight, we might judge their responses as sadly shortsighted on an occasion that should have sparked joy. Yet from the perspective of cognitive science, the apostles were actually reacting quite normally. Researchers tell us that human beings have always operated on "schemas"—mental frameworks that help organize information into familiar patterns. Schemas allow us to predict and function as we're bombarded with new data, some of which might seem "like nonsense" (Luke 24:11). *Resurrection of the body? How can that be in a world of mortality?*

Two millennia later we're blessed with Christian schemas that allow us to process the resurrection as "normal" in light of God's plan. It's complacency that threatens to blunt our response; the narrative is so familiar that we can become numb to its improbable wonder.

And so it's good, I think, that the Easter story as written reminds us every year of how extraordinary Christ's rising actually was and is from a human perspective. This is still good news with an edge—good news that perennially invites radical reframing.

**Meditation:** Did your Lenten observances encourage you to change long-worn patterns of thought and behavior? Did they help jolt you out of complacency regarding your faith? If you still feel flat, consider how you can invite in wholesome "new yeast" (cf. 1 Cor 5:7-8): exploring alternative ways to pray, reading spiritual books, getting involved in parish ministry.

**Prayer:** Loving God, invigorate my faith with the spirit of wonder during this Easter season.

## Promises of Mercy

**Readings:** Acts 2:14, 22-33; Matt 28:8-15

**Scripture:**
"I will pour out a portion of my spirit upon all flesh." (Acts 2:17 [cf. Joel 3:1])

**Reflection:** In today's reading from Acts, Luke paints a picture of a diverse first-century Jerusalem, one where the potential for misunderstandings and tensions must have been as great as in any multicultural city today. This reality adds poignancy to the unity ultimately achieved at Pentecost, as does the account's historical context. This initially contentious encounter takes place during a festival celebrating marvelous accord, the Feast of Weeks, a commemoration of God's covenant with Israel.

How far this scoffing crowd diverges from the spirit of that ancient concord as they dismiss the Holy Spirit's effect as drunkenness (Acts 2:15)! Peter is quick to remind them that speaking in tongues was prophesied by Joel, then delivers the *coup de gras*: everyone present shares guilt in the murder of God's son.

"[C]ut to the heart" (Acts 2:37), the people abruptly lose their smugness. Who could hope to atone for such monumental transgression? Peter offers a simple answer: "Repent and be baptized . . . for the forgiveness of your sins; and you will receive the gift of the Holy Spirit" (Acts 2:38).

"Do not be afraid," the resurrected Christ had told his apostles (Matt 28:10), encouraging them to shed the baggage of shame and embrace a new beginning. In that moment Peter was extending the same grace to a crowd longing to hear it, a people primed to hear it—God's mercy extended from age to age despite monumental and repeated human sin.

There was hope then. There's hope now.

**Meditation:** What would make you feel "cut to the heart" if you met Christ today? Read Scripture passages about God's covenant, including Genesis 9:8-17, Exodus 34, and the Easter Vigil readings of Isaiah 54:5-14 and Ezekiel 36:18-28. Pick a short passage that especially speaks to you, write it out, and pray with it each morning during this holy season.

**Prayer:** You are my refuge and hope, O Lord. Help me rest in your faithful covenant.

## Kindness Received and Offered

**Readings:** Acts 2:36-41; John 20:11-18

**Scripture:**
[O]f the kindness of the LORD the earth is full. (Ps 33:5)

**Reflection:** Today's Gospel brings us back to the empty tomb, where Mary Magdalene becomes the first person to encounter the risen Christ—a circumstance, certainly, for awe.

I must admit, however, that John's narrative, where Mary initially mistakes Jesus for a gardener, has always inspired me not only with awe but also with chagrin about how different my actions might have been from the gracious Mary's.

Having grown up in an eastern metropolis where people are notoriously short with each other, I'm habitually impatient, even while repeatedly vowing to reform, and even after decades in the laid-back Intermountain West. I'm reasonably sure that, given the accumulation of stressful circumstances Mary faced, this last straw of being unable to find Jesus' body would *not* have inspired me gently to call the figure "Sir" but rather to berate him in accusatory anger. How horrific it would have been, a moment later, to realize I'd just been incredibly rude to my resurrected Lord!

Popular identifications of Mary as a prostitute are mere legends, but you don't need a poignant redemption story to understand why Mary might have been predisposed to humility and kindness even under extraordinary duress. Jesus, after all, had extended remarkable kindness to her by accepting her among his closest followers. She'd repeatedly witnessed his charity and gentleness to others and had heard him affirm that God's essence is love.

Kindness, after all, is contagious. How fitting it is that Mary's response in this first showing of the risen Lord so testifies to the power of Christ's loving example!

**Meditation:** Call to mind how kindness has touched your life. Have strangers or friends offered human love and comfort? Has God led you to a place, a job, a relationship that has afforded great joy? Now reflect on times when you've found it difficult to be kind to others. What tends to trigger you to be less than charitable? How might you remember and echo divine love in such circumstances?

**Prayer:** Loving God, help me to see you in all the "gardeners" whose paths cross mine.

# Intuitive Knowing

**Readings:** Acts 3:1-10; Luke 24:13-35

**Scripture:**
[H]e was made known to them in the breaking of the bread.
(Luke 24:35)

**Reflection:** I've always believed deeply in the power of
words. As a lonely, dreaming girl, books helped me imagine
a wider, richer world. As an English professor, I saw words
guide other young people as they grew in understanding
and sympathy. As a writer, I live by words. But since I've
become a hospice massage therapist (work I've taken up in
my retirement years), I've gained a new appreciation for the
profound power of nonverbal communication. Words often
fail when people are trapped in dementia or are so ill they
cannot speak. Nevertheless, some of the most seemingly
remote patients grow less anxious on being touched with
compassionate hands, and they reflect love and gratitude
back with a hand squeeze or smile—simple actions that en-
compass worlds of meaning.

The Emmaus story certainly includes a whole lot of words
on the disciples' part. On the road these garrulous (and
rather clueless) ones tell Jesus all he ever wanted to know
about his own death and resurrection. Only later, at table,
do they recognize him, thanks to an everyday gesture that

spoke volumes: the breaking of bread, which the disciples had seen Christ do before and which evoked so many of his past teachings ("I am the bread of life," John 6:35; "This is my body, which will be given for you," Luke 22:19). The gesture was also rich with implications about the risen savior's ongoing love for them as it evoked hospitality, community, and blessings.

Words can be useful and uplifting, no doubt about it. Yet we should never forget that some of the most profound, magnificent mysteries defy them.

**Meditation:** In our hyper-rational, hyper-verbal culture, wordless, sympathetic moments of insight and connection tend to be devalued compared to reasoned-out understanding. To build the habit of noticing and celebrating this other side of human (and divine-human) communication, share with a trusted friend stories of times when you've enjoyed intuitive knowing, and invite your friend to share too. Marvel together at how "wonderfully made" (Ps 139:14) we are, to enjoy this blessed capacity.

**Prayer:** God of signs as well as words, open my eyes to your life-giving insight, however it's offered.

# Solidarity with the Suffering Christ

**Readings:** Acts 3:11-26; Luke 24:35-48

**Scripture:**
"Look at my hands and my feet, that it is I myself." (Luke 24:39)

**Reflection:** Traditionally, kings are distinguished by elaborate raiment, and messiahs are recognized by their ability to triumph over oppression. When the risen Christ appears to his assembled disciples, however, his identification as the ultimate king and messiah is confirmed by his wounds, the consequences of apparent earthly failure.

Though this might seem like a strange way to identify a leader, it is entirely fitting in Jesus' context. To confirm resurrection of the body, the disciples must see a specific, identifiable body. Such focus on brokenness also underlines that Jesus is a different kind of messiah and savior, the suffering Lamb of God, whose sacrifice delivers followers not from earthly oppression but from sin. This is a unique kind of triumph.

How out of alignment this wounded savior seems, however, from the perspective of modern popular thinking that frames God as a kind of Santa Claus: If we want (or don't want) something, all we have to do is think positively and badger God long enough! But that's nonsense, of course.

Nobody will get everything he or she desires in this mortal life. Some will be oppressed by poverty, disaster, illness, persecution; even the privileged will lose loved ones and face aging's effects. How much bleaker such experiences will be if we've been taught to understand them as signs of spiritual failure!

Jesus' broken body reminds us that we serve a king who was himself "a man of suffering, knowing pain" (Isa 53:3). Our suffering is not a self-evident indicator that he's dissatisfied with us. It's a condition that binds us all-the-more-closely to our crucified and risen Lord.

**Meditation:** What trials and wounds are you bearing? Have they made you feel less worthy or distanced you from God? In meditation or a journal, explore how they might instead be inviting you to greater solidarity with Christ. Perhaps they are drawing you toward greater compassion for others or are deepening your thirst for redemption.

**Prayer:** Help me, Lamb of God, to find in my own suffering an occasion to draw nearer to you.

## Called to Think Big

**Readings:** Acts 4:1-12; John 21:1-14

**Scripture:**
So they cast [the net], and were not able to pull it in because of the number of fish. (John 21:6)

**Reflection:** If you've ever taught, you've probably encountered students trapped in a habit of "thinking small." Though their potential may be considerable, they are all-too-ready to impose limitations on their own horizons, whether they're kindergarteners protesting "I can't DO this!" or university students gravitating to notoriously easy classes or seasoned professionals in continuing education workshops who are resisting change.

While such attitudes might be dismissed as laziness, it's important to remember that they can also result from ingrained messages about capacity. If a person hears from childhood that based on social class, gender, race, or any other reason, he or she isn't capable of doing something, those words may become a self-fulfilling prophecy.

As humble peasant fishermen, Peter and the other apostles would have been raised with a very modest sense of their own horizons. Manual workers with no opportunity for formal education, they were dismissed as mere laborers who would certainly never impact the wider world. Yet not long after Christ's death, these fishermen found themselves accomplishing astonishing feats and speaking publicly with great conviction. As if to ease them in, the first inkling of what lay ahead was communicated in the familiar setting of their occupation. ("Get it? Rethink big!" I imagine Jesus saying as they landed that exaggeratedly giant haul of fish.) Things progressed rapidly to astounding healings and a harvest of 5,000 souls.

"[F]or God all things are possible," Jesus had told them (Matt 19:26). And in those first post-resurrection weeks the previously unimaginable meaning of those words began to hit home.

Remembering the apostles' blossoming, let us also rise with confidence when God calls us to service that seems beyond our capacities, when we hear God's voice whispering, "Think bigger! I am with you."

**Meditation:** What messages about yourself have discouraged you from heeding God's call to a particular kind of service over the years? Do you feel too shy or inarticulate, lacking in knowledge or specific skills? Trust that if the call is authentic, God will provide the necessary gifts. Seek guidance, encouragement, and mentoring from others engaged in that ministry.

**Prayer:** O God, help me overcome self-doubt and rise to do your will, confident in your love.

*April 23: Saturday within the Octave of Easter*

## Manifesting Joyful Witness

**Readings:** Acts 4:13-21; Mark 16:9-15

**Scripture:**
"It is impossible for us not to speak about what we have seen and heard." (Acts 4:20)

**Reflection:** Today's "street preachers" tend to operate through media or the internet rather than on physical crossroads, but they seek to convey the same impression as those old-timers who aggressively buttonholed passersby. They've been over-whelmed by the Spirit, they'd have us believe—they can't help but testify!

There are many ways to "speak," however, as today's first reading reminds us. Under the Holy Spirit's influence the disciples lead their marketplace ministry with a "remarkable sign" (4:16) rather than a formal exhortation—a strategic choice. Healing a man who had been crippled his entire life, who jumps around praising God in a very public place, certainly gets people's attention—more than any words from these "uneducated, ordinary men" could have (4:13).

Through the centuries numerous Christians have chosen to do their preaching through their deeds, including Peter Clavier, who tended lepers, and Maximilian Kolbe, who died at Auschwitz in place of another person.

In fact you probably know someone who evangelizes with actions. I do—a woman of a certain age, an accounts clerk with no theological training, who puts her vibrant faith into action every single day. Like the disciples at the Beautiful Gate she leads with miracles, though hers are admittedly more modest. She helps tentative newcomers to our parish feel so welcome that soon they're involved in ministries; she soothes the battered spirits of those who attend the funerals where she sings. Shy about speaking (vs. singing) in public, she nevertheless manifests the glowing spirit within her, leading many back to God.

We don't have to shout and coerce to spread the good news. If others witness the power of love that animates us, they're likely to want some of that, too.

**Meditation:** Whom do you know that regularly manifests their joy in the gospel with their deeds? Pay attention to how, when, and where they do this. Rededicate yourself to "speaking" of your delight in God through your actions, and borrow from their approach.

**Prayer:** Rekindle my faith this Easter season, O Holy Spirit, that each day I may bear active witness to God's glory.

## April 24: Second Sunday of Easter
### (Sunday of Divine Mercy)

## Sharing Our Vulnerability

**Readings:** Acts 5:12-16; Rev 1:9-11a, 12-13, 17-19; John 20:19-31

**Scripture:**
Jesus came . . . and stood in their midst and said, "Peace be with you." (John 20:26)

**Reflection:** Hundreds of evacuees gathered at City Hall for information the day after a 2012 wildfire devastated my mountain neighborhood. Fueled by 40 mile-per-hour winds and 95-degree temperatures, the fire consumed 66 houses, leaving others (including mine) standing untouched as islands in a wilderness of blackened junipers and naked chimneys standing amid mounds of rubble that had been houses. Shared shock and sorrow broke down barriers that night. The haughty physician comforted the woman with five children and no insurance; the world-famous scientist commiserated with the retired railroad worker.

Barriers were also discarded on that centuries-ago day at Solomon's portico chronicled in Acts 5. As word of Peter's healing power spread and cots filled the street, mental and physical illness became very public. But not hopeless. Because those who were suffering had dared to acknowledge their need, they could be healed.

As we sit in church on Divine Mercy Sunday, we're likely to be much more guarded about our vulnerabilities. We share only with trusted friends our news about diagnoses, financial worries, loneliness, rifts, addiction, and depression. Yet we all bear burdens—even that beautiful, "perfect" Catholic family in the second pew, even the deacon and priest, even musicians like me singing so confidently (there's no other way to sing) in front of God and everybody.

Would that we might share our troubles more openly with one another as we sit together this Divine Mercy Sunday and every Sunday, each heart privately yearning for the shadow of God's healing mercy to fall upon it. Would that we could embody God's mercy for one another!

**Meditation:** Today we celebrate divine mercy as a pure gift of unearned grace, free-flowing from the heart of Jesus. Most of us, however, tend to put conditions on the mercy we dispense to others, and we resist acknowledging our vulnerability because we fear others' judgment. The next time you sense that someone is suffering, invite sharing and dedicate yourself to sympathetic, nonjudgmental listening. A trouble shared can indeed be a trouble halved.

**Prayer:** Grant me the courage, merciful God, to move beyond guardedness into loving fellowship.

*April 25: Saint Mark, Evangelist*

## Growing into Courage

**Readings:** 1 Pet 5:5b-14; Mark 16:15-20

**Scripture:**
The God of all grace . . . will himself restore, strengthen, and establish you . . . (1 Pet 5:10)

**Reflection:** A decade before I converted to Catholicism, I taught at a Catholic high school called St. Mark's near Wilmington, Delaware. The school mascot was a winged lion (as St. Mark is symbolically depicted in art), an image that struck me as particularly glorious, especially in contrast to mascots from my own high school years. The inspirational effect of my alma mater's emblem, the bear, had been decidedly blunted by our own suburb's small, shy, garbage-foraging representatives of that species. Our archrival's mascot had offered no potency at all: the Hatboro Hats (seriously). What a tradition Catholicism was, to offer such exalted symbols and empowering models!

Years later while writing a book about saints, however, I learned that although tradition highly exalts the mature St. Mark (mighty apostle, bishop of Alexandria, martyr), some commentators associate Mark in youth with New Testament figures who turned tail—the unnamed young man who shed his cloak and ran naked from Gethsemane (Mark 14:51-52), and John Mark who abandoned Peter and Barnabas when things got tough on a missionary journey (Acts 15:37-38). If these identifications are correct, the young Mark wasn't a lion but a rabbit.

At first glance such identification seems a disappointing fall. Yet arguably this backstory can make Mark a *more* helpful, more identifiable model. Few of us are born winged lions, after all; we panic, waiver, and disappoint. If we learn, however, to say "Thy will be done," God can work potently glorious marvels in us, providing resolve to the tentative, even inspiring courage in the cowardly.

He's the one, after all, who supplies the wings.

**Meditation:** Learning to trust God, to heed his call and walk into difficult situations when our instincts are urging flight, certainly isn't easy. When have you run away, fearful and determined to save yourself? What circumstances daunt you now? Take inspiration from the stories of saints such as Mark who learned after imperfect and nervous beginnings to trust that God would "restore, strengthen, and establish" them.

**Prayer:** Let me live my life with courage, O God, relying securely on your faithful power.

## Selflessly Sharing Resources

**Readings:** Acts 4:32-37; John 3:7b-15

**Scripture:**
[N]o one claimed that any of his possessions was his own
. . . (Acts 4:32)

**Reflection:** Acts 4 is clear: the earliest Christians "had every-thing in common" (v. 32) and distributed their wealth and property "to each according to need" (v. 35). Soon, though, that way of life disappeared from church history, monasteries and utopian communities aside. This evolution might suggest that sharing everything with others just isn't workable for most people in the long-term; we're innately a self-protective species with tendencies toward freeloading and feeling aggrieved.

Yet those first Christians were human, too, beset (as the New Testament tells us) by rivalries, jealousies, and temptations, just as we are. And they were possessed of fewer re-sources. So how did they do it? Perhaps they took to heart Jesus' assurance that God would provide everything they needed, just as he did for the birds of the air (Matt 6:25-34). Perhaps the example of the traveling-light apostles sustained them. Perhaps, anticipating an imminent second coming, they simply told themselves that they could do anything for a little while.

What I do know is that these early Christian communities call us to attention whenever our hands convulsively grip a resource that seems in short supply (*mine!*) rather than sharing it with others. At the moment my own thinnest resource is time, and just yesterday I put off someone who needs my care. "Maybe next weekend," I told her.

As I write at dawn this Tuesday morning, though, I find myself imagining what it might be like to act as if I really did believe that God knows what I need—a second wind, more energy—and will provide it.

"I'll see you at 5:00 tonight," I email her, taking a deep breath, willing my hands to open.

**Meditation:** Consider giving from a nonmonetary resource you feel is already limited in your life. Maybe that's time; maybe it's emotional energy. Can you offer relief breaks to a caregiver for a spouse with dementia? Can you take time to help others with tax preparation or tend the parish garden? Selfless sharing can make a church community feel like family.

**Prayer:** Sustain me with what I need, Holy Spirit, as I share my gifts with others.

*April 27: Wednesday of the Second Week of Easter*

## Making the Way Straight

**Readings:** Acts 5:17-26; John 3:16-21

**Scripture:**
But during the night, the angel of the Lord opened the doors
of the prison . . . (Acts 5:19)

**Reflection:** "I was floored when I got the call." My friend
smiles, her long-ago joy brightly remembered. "I'd been
trying to get my head around the fact that it might never
happen, obsessing over alternatives but not coming up with
anything. I was in mourning—but premature mourning, as
it turned out." She'd long dreamed of working in the Peace
Corps, but so many young people had applied in that ide-
alistic era that she'd been waitlisted and told not to get her
hopes up. Much time had passed. Then the phone rang, and
she was plunged into a whirl of preparation for a posting in
a rural African elementary school, work that inspired a lifelong vocation.

When Isaiah says to "prepare the way of the LORD" (40:3;
an admonition John the Baptist repeats in John 1:23), he's
instructing humans to facilitate God's work. Sometimes,
though, the Lord graciously steps in to make *our* ways straight,
removing apparently stout obstacles in remarkably timely
fashion. This work of God is attested by today's first reading,

as well as by many saints' lives, my friend's example, and no doubt your own experience.

How glorious the new enterprise feels when that happens—often more glorious than if the obstacle had not appeared in the first place. In such moments God's grace feels very personal, and the once-blocked way seems an incredible, almost inconceivable, gift.

I imagine that the apostles must have felt similarly "radiant with joy," as today's psalm says (34:6), ever more confirmed in their sense of purpose as they emerged from prison to teach in the temple area, glowing with contagious faith.

**Meditation:** Set aside some time today to remember and celebrate an instance when God opened a door for you. Refresh your sense of joy and wonder by replaying detailed memories of your initial frustration and sadness, of the moment the obstacle vanished, of the grace you felt on beginning, and of the good things that have resulted.

**Prayer:** I will praise you, Lord, for you have rescued me!

## Courageous Truth-Telling and Its Fruits

**Readings:** Acts 5:27-33; John 3:31-36

**Scripture:**
"We must obey God rather than men." (Acts 5:29)

**Reflection:** How far Peter has come from the fearful man who denied Jesus three times! How different the apostles are from the men hiding after the crucifixion! No longer afraid of punishment for being identified with Jesus, they stand courageously before the high court, fortified by encounters with the risen Lord and the descent of the Holy Spirit at Pentecost. Exemplifying righteous civil disobedience, they assert their responsibility to tell Jesus' truth, defying the Sanhedrin.

A governing council of elders, the Sanhedrin was a supreme court, the final authority on Jewish law, both civil and religious. The council was powerful, and challenging its authority could be dangerous. Yet the apostles did challenge this powerful assembly with courage that foreshadowed not only their own martyrdom, but generations of martyrs to come. This is courage before which we ordinary Christians can only stand in awe.

In today's world we're bombarded by people who claim the role of heroic truth-teller defying a corrupt order, outspoken ones from across the political spectrum. We're challenged to evaluate which of them are obeying God ("obeying" in Hebrew also means "listening to") and which will lead us astray.

Fortunately now, as two thousand years ago, Jesus' own words offer guidance: "By their fruits you will know them" (Matt 7:16). Does a speaker ultimately promote love of neighbor, service to the poor, forgiveness, personal humility before God? Does his or her life mirror these principles?

If not, the "truth" being told is not the apostles' good news.

**Meditation:** Read the words and life stories of brave ones who have spoken out publicly in the face of personal danger (perhaps Óscar Romero, Martin Luther King Jr., or Mahatma Gandhi). Let them inspire you and provide models for truth-telling that are both effective and in accordance with gospel principles. What necessary truth might you be called to tell? Who needs to hear it? What potential fruits might such telling yield?

**Prayer:** Help me, Jesus, to be courageous in speaking for you and wise in discerning as I weigh others' words.

*April 29: Saint Catherine of Siena,*
*Virgin and Doctor of the Church*

## From Little, Much

**Readings:** Acts 5:34-42; John 6:1-15

**Scripture:**
"There is a boy here who has five barley loaves and two fish; but what good are these for so many?" (John 6:9)

**Reflection:** "It's wonderful that you visit her," I tell a parish hospital minister outside an elderly patient's room. "She loves your company."

She protests, saying she feels like she contributes so little— just conversation and companionship twice a week. "I wish I could help her like you can," she says. "Her stiff neck is always so much better after the massages, and she feels her heartbeat and breath easing, and she sleeps better after you've come."

I shake my head, smiling ruefully, because lately I've been imagining that I make only a pathetically small difference compared to the hospice nurses who are my coworkers. Come to think of it, they probably have days, too, when they envy the particular talents of other nurses and doctors—or even wish, now and then, that their tight schedules allowed them to offer the more leisurely kinds of comfort that hospital ministers and hospice massage therapists can provide.

The fact is that each of us brings specific, particular skills to this business of doing God's work in the world—talents that individually might seem so small but together yield rich results.

Today's readings show God repeatedly and magnificently multiplying the reach of individuals' efforts. We hear of the apostles, whose witness spread faith to thousands, and the boy by the Sea of Galilee, whose modest offering practically became a Costco. These are stories to remember, indeed, on those days when we feel discouraged about the smallness of our own contributions.

Christ has long been in the business, after all, of making much from little.

**Meditation:** Call to mind someone whose service might seem modest but who feeds others in extraordinary ways. Pray for the grace to encourage and cheer that person, and write a note of thanks chronicling the contribution in detail (specific examples really stick with people!).

**Prayer:** Gracious Christ, let me never forget that you're eager to multiply my gifts. Let me offer them with confidence to you.

## Sharing Authority

**Readings:** Acts 6:1-7; John 6:16-21

**Scripture:**
The proposal was acceptable to the whole community . . .
(Acts 6:5)

**Reflection:** Not only did members of the new Christian community share possessions; its leaders also shared authority, perhaps an even rarer phenomenon. More typically, those at the top tend to rule absolutely, driven by a desire for power and the feeling that they know what's best. "*Somebody* has to be in charge," those who lead have been known to protest when, in crisis mode, we tighten our grip on the reins (ask me how I know).

In today's first reading the Twelve face their own crisis. Tensions flare over charity extended to widows, a highly symbolic and sensitive issue given the community's mix of Jewish and Gentile believers. If the center is to hold, leaders cannot appear to be favoring those of their own tradition, nor can they appear to privilege the converts.

The solution seems directly inspired by the Holy Spirit, affirming the ethos of mutual love and respect so central to Christianity. The apostles delegate, giving everyone a say in choosing individuals from among them to alleviate the issue. The community's size undoubtedly encourages multiple points of view, but they come to a decision. Ratifying the choice of seven believers with a blessing, the apostles implicitly emphasize that a loving God should be the point of reference for any action.

No wonder the cause of Christianity prospered and "the number of the disciples . . . increased greatly" (6:7), given the lack of leader-ego represented in this resolution. The Twelve set an example that accorded with what they proclaimed: the Holy Spirit's wisdom lives in all believers, so all should be offered a voice as God's children.

**Meditation:** Leadership positions come in all shapes and sizes, from directing nations and municipalities; to overseeing businesses, nonprofits, and departments; to influencing clubs and informal groups of friends; to organizing and nurturing family members. Pick one setting where you're a leader and make an honest review of your practice. Where might you better enhance a sense of community and honor God's presence in others by listening and collaborating?

**Prayer:** Help me be the kind of leader, O God, who willingly and lovingly shares authority.

## Guilt and Grace

**Readings:** Acts 5:27-32, 40b-41; Rev 5:11-14; John 21:1-19 or 21:1-14

**Scripture:**
"Yes, Lord, you know that I love you." (John 21:15)

**Reflection:** I believed myself a criminally inept caregiver as my husband was dying young of cancer twenty years ago. Despite deep love and fervent intentions, my words, deeds, and demeanor never seemed right. After he died guilt morphed to self-loathing and depression. *Others instinctively know what to do, but you failed.* One night in a dream I met my beloved in the afterlife—and he turned his back.

Only last year, speaking at a conference for family caregivers, did I realize the folly of embracing this destructive way of thinking. Hearing the stories of hundreds who were called to serve loved ones ill, disabled, and dying, I realized that there'd been nothing unusual about my caregiving—or my guilt. Everyone attending was similarly convinced that he or she had been the world's worst caregiver. Everyone struggled with shame over minor, unintentional trespasses.

Today's Gospel, with its story of incredible forgiveness, offers shining hope for all whose lives are blighted by a sense of having let another down.

Peter's betrayal was of a different degree entirely than a caregiver's clumsy lapses, involving as it did three voluntary denials on the crucifixion's eve. Thus, as he later rushes to meet the risen Christ on the shore, his delight must have been mixed with at least some apprehension. If a moment ever deserved a turned back! Rather than castigating, however, Jesus gently, firmly "rewinds" Peter's denials in an almost ritualistic, purgative way. He invites three public affirmations of love, folding Peter into ongoing relationship with admonitions to "Feed my sheep" and "Follow me" (21:17, 19).

I suspect I'm not the only person mourning a loved one who's teared up when this reading comes around, who's dreamed that such grace might also extend to me.

**Meditation:** What regrets do you have in regard to your past conduct toward others that can't be fixed because of their passing? Were words foolishly spoken or left unspoken? What actions done or left undone haunt you? Meditate on Peter's experience in a quiet place, asking forgiveness of God and your loved one, praying for the grace to forgive yourself.

**Prayer:** Merciful Christ, help me move past guilt and hear your call to new service.

## God-Inspired Beauty

**Readings:** Acts 6:8-15; John 6:22-29

**Scripture:**
[H]is face was like the face of an angel. (Acts 6:15)

**Reflection:** No one would have called her physically beautiful, that aged nun who became my friend during the most difficult summer of my life. On retreat at a Benedictine convent as a new widow, I'd been afforded daily counseling with an insightful, highly qualified sister, and I spent many hours in a library consulting books on death, grief, and spirituality. In retrospect, though, the deepest, most blessed salve came from Sister Dorothy, an aged gardener of simple faith.

Tiny, wizened, her face marked from a congenital cleft palate, speaking with the heavy German accent of her childhood, Dorothy bustled up to me in the refectory that first evening as if she'd been divinely directed. "Sit with me," she insisted. When she discovered that I too loved gardening, she invited me to work beside her in the afternoons among the raspberries, flowers, and herbs. Such physical distraction comingled with Dorothy's patient listening presence proved exactly what I needed, and as I returned on retreat each subsequent summer, the sight of her felt like the apprehension of an angel.

As a young woman Dorothy had been denied entry into another convent because of her flawed face. How conclusively those rigid perfectionists had missed the whole point of community life!

We don't know what Stephen really looked like, but that doesn't matter; what does matter is that believers beheld him as having the face of an angel, thanks to the Holy Spirit's radiant presence in his glowing soul.

Let us be wise, able to recognize and respond to God-inspired beauty in people we meet, whatever their appearance.

**Meditation:** Who have been the angels in your life, those endowed with divinely inspired beauty, those who God employed to support and comfort you? Pray in thanksgiving for the blessing of their lives and consider how you might imitate their actions and their spirit when you meet someone in need.

**Prayer:** Heavenly Father, grant me the grace to become a beautiful witness of your love to others.

*May 3: Saints Philip and James, Apostles*

# The Limits of Comprehension

**Readings:** 1 Cor 15:1-8; John 14:6-14

**Scripture:**
"How can you say, 'Show us the Father'?" (John 14:8)

**Reflection:** I'll admit it: as someone who taught writing to college students for forty years, my standards for homilies are perhaps a little too rigorous. I'm always disappointed when a preacher dodges a challenging passage in Scripture and resorts to platitudes; I'm discouraged when biblical scholarship is left unapplied. I imagine what I might say, were I given the chance.

Such vainglory utterly vanishes, however, when the reading's subject is the Trinity—that concept so rife with obscure theological terms, so resistant to human logic! *Better you than me*, I thought recently, as I watched students in a religious education class pressing our priest for a simpler explanation. "Look," Father Isaac finally said, drawing himself up to his whole 5'6" height and decisively raising his hand. "It's a mystery! You can't explain it! You just have to believe it!"

Today's Gospel demonstrates that even those who knew Jesus personally struggled to comprehend a multi-person Godhead, as Philip does at the Last Supper. "Have I been with you for so long . . . and you still do not know me . . . ?" Jesus asks with frustration (John 14:9). Then, taking pity, he offers an out: if they can't grasp the idea, they should "believe because of the works themselves" (14:11).

This is both an inspired concession to the limits of human understanding and an incredibly sensible tool for those disciples who will soon be teaching the faith. In those streets there will be no leisure for dense philosophical inquiry—in fact, it would be distracting.

Sometimes you just have to believe.

**Meditation:** Have you ever been confronted by an atheist who demanded that you explain a part of your faith that's inherently mysterious, then derided you when you couldn't do so? When you chide yourself for not understanding the incomprehensible, turn to saints who lacked or struggled with esoteric learning but grew rich in understanding through grace and faith, such as St. John Vianney and St. Bernadette.

**Prayer:** Triune God, let my works speak of your incomprehensible, mysterious glory when logic fails. Help me to believe when I cannot prove.

## Compelled to New Pastures

**Readings:** Acts 8:1b-8; John 6:35-40

**Scripture:**
Now those who had been scattered went about preaching the word. (Acts 8:4)

**Reflection:** After Stephen's martyrdom, it "gets real" for the new Christians. Certainly the apostles knew, given Christ's prophecy and suffering, that their mission would be dangerous. But now the risk comes home as persecution succeeds rancor and believers are scattered.

Jesus' followers could have given up. Instead they trust the Holy Spirit and take their message to the hinterlands, performing healing miracles and converting those who are willing to listen.

Two thousand years later, to our shame, there was much more resisting and whining when a parish community I belonged to was scattered. Our 1990s "persecution" only involved the demotion of our beloved campus church from parish to student center—not a physical threat—but the matter was badly handled. Instead of being upfront, the powers-that-were demanded a lengthy report detailing the state of the parish—one that took months to prepare and revealed a thriving enterprise but was immediately brushed aside and disregarded.

After we were told to scatter to the city's other churches, a few especially bitter members simply quit organized religion; several became Unitarians. Most of us, though, found our way into local parishes sooner or later. It felt so strange, at first, to worship in these more traditional settings among strangers! Yet those strangers proved eager for our fresh perspectives and gifts, and over the decades we have become mainstays of liturgy committees, parish councils, ministries of word and music, and catechesis, deeply enriching these "new pastures" (to borrow John Milton's phrase).

Diaspora is painful, for sure. But sometimes it seems to be exactly what the Holy Spirit has in mind.

**Meditation:** Think about a past situation that compelled you to leave familiar surroundings and begin anew elsewhere. Did you feel fearful and abandoned? Did you resist? Have you been able to reframe a mission that seemed threatened, carrying it to a new place? Thinking back, what gifts has the Holy Spirit drawn from the situation?

**Prayer:** Sustain me when things change, O Holy Spirit. Let me trust that I'm being led to rich new work.

*May 5: Thursday of the Third Week of Easter*

## Obeying Orders

**Readings:** Acts 8:26-40; John 6:44-51

**Scripture:**
The Spirit said to Phillip, "Go and join up with that chariot."
(Acts 8:29)

**Reflection:** Today's first reading offers a scene apparently so over-the-top unlikely and fast-evolving that it verges on madcap. Imagine the eunuch's perspective: you're peacefully riding along, puzzling over a book, and suddenly this guy comes out of nowhere—just the right guy, it so happens, to help you understand the book—and you just know you have to be baptized right now, though the idea hasn't previously crossed your mind.

The backstory, of course, changes things. This wasn't a random encounter; an angel directed Phillip to that very road and ordered him to chase down that specific chariot.

This morning I shivered upon discovering that this was today's theme, remembering how the other day I myself heard an irresistible call to "go"—one that might have made me seem forward and inappropriate.

I was visiting a silent elderly woman in the early stages of dementia. She dozed as I gave her a gentle comfort-touch massage. Midway through the session an overwhelming urge came to me: *Sing to her as you work.* Though feeling tired and a bit shy that afternoon, I complied. Because nothing in her room indicated whether or not she was a church-lady, I chose gentle folksongs and forties classics, but as the session's end neared, I yielded to the sudden compulsion to sing "Be Still, My Soul."

As my hands lifted from her body, her eyes opened and she smiled. "Oh, honey," she said. "It's been so long since I've been to church. That's my favorite, and it's such a comfort to remember those words now."

"Jump!" the Holy Spirit still says to us today. We ignore those promptings at our peril.

**Meditation:** Dedicate yourself today to listening for promptings that involve "putting yourself out there" but have the potential to serve another. If the situation is safe, take the risk to act without overthinking, trusting in a God who is perpetually tapping us on the shoulder, saying, "Go."

**Prayer:** Help me to hear your voice, Holy Spirit, and give me the willingness to act as you inspire me.

## May 6: Friday of the Third Week of Easter

## Reoriented from Rigidity to Meekness

**Readings:** Acts 9:1-20; John 6:52-59

**Scripture:**
Immediately things like scales fell from his eyes and he regained his sight. (Acts 9:18)

**Reflection:** "A rigid young man," Pope Francis termed the pre-conversion Paul in a morning homily in 2017. Broadening his message to all who engage in ideological, self-righteous clinging to the forms of religion, Francis counseled that those who believe themselves exemplary for following the letter of the law need to think again.

What a necessary message this is! Though insisting dogmatically on time-honored ways is often associated with aging (*I don't like that new liturgy!*), it can infect us at any stage of life, especially at times when we long for clarity and the easy comfort of absolute "dos and don'ts" in social interactions, at work, and in faith life. Young adults as rigid as Paul still exist. Recently a campus minister friend reported with a rueful smile how two of her charges warned her that contemplative meditation was a "pagan" danger to her soul!

Naturally, given our desire to be good—even perfect—people, we welcome the reassurance of clear guidelines, the disciplines that instruct us in the right way. Sometimes, though, God demands flexibility, exceptions.

In today's first reading Ananias doesn't understand this when he initially resists meeting Paul, clinging to entrenched attitudes despite a heavenly vision—*once an enemy of the Lord, always an enemy of the Lord*. His eventual obedience meant that Paul was not the only person who learned to see the world anew that day.

Meekness, Pope Francis said in the same homily, is the antithesis of rigidity, and Christ's new covenant calls us to the meekness of love. May we recall that whenever our eyes begin to self-righteously cloud.

**Meditation:** In what ways might you be clinging to rigid, comfortably "righteous" ways? Meditate on moments in Christ's life which embody new paradigms: mixing with sinners (Mark 2:16-17), not condemning others who transgressed the law (John 8:1-11), honoring inner intentions vs. outward display (Matt 5:21-48). Where might you dare to open to new, Christ-inspired ways of fulfilling God's commandments?

**Prayer:** Lord of love, meet me on my life's road whenever I need conversion, turning my heart from self-righteousness to meekness, from blindness to sight.

## An Ordinary, Extraordinary Woman

**Readings:** Acts 9:31-42; John 6:60-69

**Scripture:**
He gave her his hand and raised her up . . . (Acts 9:41)

**Reflection:** Today we hear of another miraculous rebirth soon after Paul's own change of heart, but one with evocative differences. This rebirth isn't a realization; it's a literal bodily reversal of death. Its subject isn't a powerful man who will star in Acts as his words shake the world, but an ordinary Christian woman, someone on whom the biblical spotlight shines just this once.

Yet Tabitha (also known as Dorcas) is extraordinary, too, in her own way. A local leader working heroically on behalf of poor widows (sewing all those garments by hand must have taken forever), Tabitha is so precious to the community that her death shakes Joppa, and her miraculous return to life inspires many baptisms. She is one of only two people raised by the apostles in Acts, and her raising from the dead comes first.

Faithful women are securely on God's radar, Tabitha's story confirms, deserving of highest honors as they contribute the time-consuming labor that might seem minor in movers' and shakers' eyes but constitutes the core work of tending Christ's sheep. What a blessed gift her example offers to women who work today in such behind-the-scenes support roles as social service and church office staff, parish committee members, altar-cloth washers, etc.!

Let us always remember that God registers our service no matter how inconspicuous, and that he's perfectly capable of reaching in and using the circumstances of our lives—whether dramatically as with Tabitha, or in ways we may never know—for our good, others' good, even the good of all his holy church.

**Meditation:** Do you know someone whose life echoes Tabitha's, a woman who works quietly, tirelessly, and selflessly for others? How has this person enriched those around her on a daily basis? What broader effects has that work yielded? Remembering that we all need emotional resurrection now and then, let her know that she's seen and appreciated.

**Prayer:** Resurrected Jesus, when I grow tired in your service or feel invisible in my work, revive me in energy and hope.

*May 8: Fourth Sunday of Easter*

## Knowing When to Walk Away

**Readings:** Acts 13:14, 43-52; Rev 7:9, 14b-17; John 10:27-30

**Scripture:**
So they shook the dust from their feet . . . and went to Iconium. (Acts 13:51)

**Reflection:** All helping professionals occasionally encounter "hard cases," people who steadfastly resist even the gentlest, most reasonable suggestions for their benefit. "But I *like* fast food," a man housebound by severe health issues insisted to my home-health nurse friend. "That's *my* business!"

In such situations it's tempting to keep insisting, growing more frustrated in the process, until the situation becomes a potentially explosive contest of wills.

The story of the apostles at Antioch of Pisidia offers a different paradigm for responding to obdurate resistance. Paul and others had done their best to bring Christ's message to the Jewish community in Antioch, but ears stayed deaf. The situation's danger intensified.

So, like Kenny Rogers's gambler (sorry, but it's so fitting), the apostles know "when to fold 'em" and "when to walk away," shaking the dust from their feet without recriminations or regrets, turning to a more promising field.

Contemporary psychiatry would applaud such action as healthy behavior under the circumstances. Research shows that people who stubbornly persist after it becomes clear that an enterprise is doomed invite crippling anger and/or depression. Refusing to admit obvious defeat wastes effort that might be applied in other ways.

And what a difference the apostles made, when at the Holy Spirit's direction they transferred their focus and moved on!

There are important lessons here about overcoming ego and letting God lead—lessons we've heard before in Acts, lessons we will hear again.

**Meditation:** The tricky thing about the lesson above, of course, is gauging whether the situation is truly hopeless and you've done all you can, or if you're quitting prematurely. The key is being honest with yourself and asking God for guidance. Are there additional efforts you might make to solve the problem? Or has persistence started to become a matter of ego? How might God be calling you to invest your labors more fruitfully?

**Prayer:** O Lord, who guided the apostles' steps, give me the wisdom to discern when it's time for me to bless something or someone and move on.

## No East or West

**Readings:** Acts 11:1-18; John 10:1-10

**Scripture:**
"As I began to speak, the Holy Spirit fell upon them as it had upon us in the beginning . . ." (Acts 11:15)

**Reflection:** Though external persecution posed a frightening challenge to early Christianity, an internal dilemma—the question of group definition—was arguably even more threatening. Were Jesus' followers to consider themselves Jews operating under a new covenant? If so, how Jewish were they to be regarding laws and customs? Or was this to be a new religion altogether, one where the divisions between Gentile and Jew had disappeared?

Multiple stories in Acts describe how believers worked out the specifics of this question. Should apostles eat with Gentiles who did not keep Jewish dietary laws? Must Gentiles be circumcised if they wanted to become Christians? Discussion over such identity markers could even become heated, leading, for example, to the council in Jerusalem described in Acts 15.

Today we might dismiss this obsessing over identity markers as ancient tribalism. Yet as I write, our nation is gripped by the consequences of its own tribalism, shaken with protest as calls sound for police reform, racial equality, and justice.

We've long termed ourselves "one nation under God," and yet we remain divided.

I dream that as you're reading these words in the future, all will be treated as brothers and sisters. As someone who witnessed 1960s idealism yield to greed and continued injustice, though, my hopes aren't too high. People just naturally seem to view their own ways as superior, the other's as suspicious.

Would that we might really listen to Jesus' own radical message of inclusive fellowship, one that came home to Peter when the Holy Spirit possessed the Gentiles in his presence.

Would that as God's family we could let the identity politics go and grant that "in Christ there is no east or west," as the sweet old hymn says, the fire of love rekindled in our hearts.

**Meditation:** Notice today when tribalism and prejudice arise around you or within you. Reach across a boundary with an act of fellowship as testimony that the Holy Spirit lives in you.

**Prayer:** God of love, make me a channel of your peace when divisions shake the family of your people.

*May 10: Tuesday of the Fourth Week of Easter*

## Relaxing into God's Love

**Readings:** Acts 11:19-26; John 10:22-30

**Scripture:**
"My sheep hear my voice; I know them, and they follow me." (John 10:27)

**Reflection:** As Easter neared the year I converted to Catholicism, anxiety drove me to come clean with my spiritual director. I assured him that the liturgies moved me deeply, making me feel closer to God than ever before. The theology was profound and compelling. I loved the community. Yet when I considered my rebellious tendencies, my inclination toward hyper-rational analytical mental operations, and my character flaws, I wondered whether I really belonged. "Look, Susan," he replied, smiling, "It's obvious to all of us that this is your path. Take a deep breath and understand that if God didn't want you, he wouldn't have given you the desire to seek him."

That was the afternoon I first heard the word "scruples," and since then I've realized that my case was comparatively mild. For those with even stronger perfectionist leanings, though, persistent feelings of spiritual unworthiness can even become psychiatric illness.

Today's Gospel offers a particularly lovely version of the sentiment my spiritual director so kindly uttered that day.

It reminds us that we become Jesus' followers not by earning the privilege as perfect models but because through grace the shepherd has already chosen us, called us by our particular names. If he hadn't, we wouldn't have any interest in his voice.

Whenever we worry about our inherent flaws or question our fundamental worthiness to be members of this flock, this fact offers so much relief. God already loves us, already has faith in us. To long for God is in itself evidence of our belonging.

Let us resolutely quiet our insecurity and relax in trust, putting our energy into serving him.

**Meditation:** Non-Catholics joke about the sacrament of reconciliation as evidence of Catholicism's supposed obsession with guilt, but if you've experienced it, you know how transcendently liberating it can be. We come relying on God's mercy; we leave washed clean. If you're feeling unworthy right now, seek the shepherd's voice in reconciliation, a celebration of God's faithful love.

**Prayer:** Shepherd God, I thank you always and everywhere for choosing me as your own. Help me to rest securely in your love.

## Coordinated Teamwork

**Readings:** Acts 12:24–13:5a; John 12:44-50

**Scripture:**
[T]hey laid hands on them and sent them off. (Acts 13:3)

**Reflection:** One of the most delightful sections of Handel's Messiah word-paints Isaiah 53:6 as the chorus and orchestra break into gleeful polyphonic repetition of the text: "We have turned, everyone to his own way." The energy is wonderful, as voices overlap and jostle for dominance, each part dancing to its own drummer. The only unfortunate consequence? For listeners, the words get lost.

I try to remember that chorus as a corrective every time I grimace at yet another ministry training that feels like micromanaging—those music ministry meetings, for instance, where we're all told to sing the same song for sending forth at every Mass in the season to come.

Yet liturgical and catechetical consistency is crucial. If every minister in every ministry "turned to his own way," we'd risk exuberant near-chaos as hard to follow as that chorus's. If congregants are to anticipate what's coming next and focus on substance, liturgy must function as consistent ritual. Glaring differences that invite someone in the assembly to think, "Oh, good, this is the one who does it the way I like!" put too much emphasis on us and can be divisive.

Today's Gospel emphasizes the apostles' care to coordinate their efforts and validate each other in the spirit of cooperative teamwork. Paul—the charismatic outsider—touches base in Jerusalem. He and Barnabas don't just wander off to Cyprus; they're commissioned by peers in Antioch. These leaders understand that they must present and embody a unified front if the new faith is to spread.

Yes, we ministers today have the right and responsibility to share our ideas and preferences. Ultimately, though, we too must be willing to coordinate as a team for the common good.

**Meditation:** Is there an element of church ritual or practice whose significance you don't understand as a minister or parishioner? Ask adult religious education leaders at your church to present a workshop explaining the "why" of this community practice. Be open to what you can learn.

**Prayer:** Bless me with discipline and a cooperative spirit, O God, as I seek to serve your church.

## A New Concept of Lineage

**Readings:** Acts 13:13-25; John 13:16-20

**Scripture:**
"I know those whom I have chosen." (John 13:18)

**Reflection:** In today's world most of us are likely to draw upon personal accomplishments to establish our authority—our degrees, our job and service experience, our awards and successful children. In the case of biblical Israel, though, as in many past times and cultures, what mattered wasn't what you'd done, but who you were in terms of family lineage. Key positions in Jewish religious life were hereditary; to be a priest, for example, you had to show descent from Aaron. Land was inherited based on ancestral family identification. Those unable to document their lineage were second-class citizens both legally and culturally.

When synagogue listeners resist Paul's message, he therefore naturally invokes Jesus' ancestry, tracing Christ's patrimony through David's line, framing Jesus as a savior from the most illustrious line of descent imaginable.

Among themselves, though, Christ's followers were even then growing into a radical new understanding of "family." Jesus' words and the Holy Spirit's promptings guided them to see that what confers the honor of being an insider isn't tribal genetics and family tree, but Christ's choice of a person as one of his sheep. Hereditary bona fides are irrelevant.

That new standard of worth changed everything for the early Gentile converts, and for all who have followed Jesus since then.

You might come from a family with no roots in any faith at all. You might have been born and raised in humble circumstances. You might not boast an eye-popping resume. If you claim Jesus' patronage, though, you're touched with royal authority.

**Meditation:** What accomplishments do you trot out when you feel insecure or overlooked, eager to establish that you should be listened to? Or do you rely on reflected glory from your genealogy or some other life experience to bolster your sense that you're somebody to be taken seriously? The next time such a moment comes, focus instead on joyful moments of unity with Christ and evidence of his faithful covenant with you.

**Prayer:** Holy Father, let my strongest refuge and dearest boast always be in my relationship with you.

## A Noah's Ark of Characters

**Readings:** Acts 13:26-33; John 14:1-6

**Scripture:**
"In my Father's house there are many dwelling places."
(John 14:2)

**Reflection:** My late husband enjoyed general faculty meetings at our university not for the predictable administrative orations or often-contentious discussions, but for (as he put it) the "Noah's Ark-style" assembly of faculty. Friendly, common-sense geologists; introverted, brilliant mathematicians; professors of modern dance, accounting, and history; master oboists, nurses, and surveyors; philosophers and pharmacists—what a good reminder of the rich legacy of human learning a university can transmit, he'd remark, and of the dazzling variety of ways people can "be smart."

The Easter season readings, so full of varied characters, attest that from earliest days the church also honored the distinctive individual personalities so essential for its functioning. Paul is a brilliant preacher, but he requires locally connected disciples in Antioch for practical support. Tabitha's private ministry to poor widows bodies-forth Jesus' spirit of charity. Converts plying practical occupations supply funding. Martyrs give inspiration. The variety of saints in subsequent centuries underlines this "many dwelling places" theme. Imagine the intellectual Thomas Aquinas sitting between the wild desert hermit St. Pelagia the Penitent and the sweet, unlettered doorkeeper Blessed André Bessette in a heavenly faculty meeting.

The commemoration of Our Lady of Fatima, which falls on this day, offers its own reminder that all kinds of people have key roles to play in Christianity. That 1917 apparition of the Virgin Mary came to three shepherd children whose gifts of innocence and simple faith helped them see what the powerful and wise could not. It sparked a renaissance of faith during the World War I era, when the world so desperately needed reassurance of divine presence.

We all have places prepared for us; we are all called by our particular names.

**Meditation:** What room in God's house are you occupying, responding with particular personality traits to the up-building of the kingdom? Has that calling changed during your life? Is it now evolving? If you find yourself without a room or "dwelling place" and are unsure how to contribute, ask a trusted friend or spiritual director for guidance.

**Prayer:** Heavenly Father, help me to understand how my particular talents might best serve you. Help me also to celebrate others' distinctiveness.

## Self-Interest and Love

**Readings:** Acts 1:15-17, 20-26; John 15:9-17

**Scripture:**
"This I command you: love one another." (John 15:17)

**Reflection:** What a pervasive theme love is in Christianity—from 1 Corinthians to folksy aphorisms ("The best way to find love is to find God") to hymns ("They'll know we are Christians by our love"). Pledging ourselves to kindness, patience, bearing with, bearing up, etc., is integral to following Jesus.

Spend a few hours in the everyday world, however, and you'll be reminded just how difficult "loving one another" truly is. Strangers, acquaintances, friends, even loved ones do the darndest things—inappropriate things that irritate everyone, grumpy or hostile actions that make patience hard to muster. Even in monasteries, seminaries, and parish offices, people get on each other's nerves. What's a well-intentioned Christian to do?

In that context it's interesting to consider the character in Acts 1:15-26: Mr. *Almost*-an-Apostle, Joseph called Barsabbas. He must have been an extraordinary man to have been shortlisted for Judas's replacement. He might have been dreaming of great things. But he lost the lottery.

If that had happened to me, I might have tried some creative bargaining: *"Why does it have to be twelve? Why not both/and?"* We have no record of how Joseph Barsabbas himself responded, however. Was he angry? Did he quit the whole Jesus movement? Did he persist, summoning Christ's spirit in order to move beyond jealousy and into the *agape*-style love that lets bygones be bygones? Did he perhaps even become the brave apostle referenced later in Antioch with Paul (Acts 15:22-23) or the legendary bishop/martyr of Eleutheropolis?

What would you have done? Where is your response on this continuum between self-absorption and love?

**Meditation:** "Stand up for yourself!" our culture insists to those who feel slighted. If you're struggling with maintaining Christian love in such circumstances, it can help to consult the examples of saints who were not accorded their due by fellow believers yet maintained patient gentleness—perhaps Padre Pio or Jeanne Jugan—meditating on how they reflected Jesus' graciousness.

**Prayer:** Help me, O God, to grow into a mature Christ-based understanding of love. Give me the resolve to persist in its spirit when things don't go my way.

*May 15: Fifth Sunday of Easter*

## Heroic Perseverance

**Readings:** Acts 14:21-27; Rev 21:1-5a; John 13:31-33a, 34-35

**Scripture:**
They strengthened the spirits of the disciples and exhorted them to persevere in the faith . . . (Acts 14:22)

**Reflection:** Upon reading the lists of exotic places in Asia Minor and Europe that the apostles visited, modern readers might find themselves skimming, thinking vaguely, "Wow, they really did get around!" The route described in today's first reading, however, deserves deeper contemplation, for its details emphasize the indomitable spirit these men brought to their work.

As biblical historians note, the easiest way to complete that first missionary journey would have been to travel overland from the final destination, Derbe, to the port of Tarsus and sail for Antioch. Instead, Paul and Barnabas elect to reprise their outward-bound route, trekking back through the brand-new Christian communities they've established in order to offer follow-up administrative and inspirational help. Not only are they investing more time, they're courting danger by returning to the very places where they've already encountered resistance and persecution.

I marvel at this story, knowing how deeply I crave home after a long trip, even a pleasant one. I'm also all too aware of the temptation to let good enough be good enough and the tendency to shrink from experiences that once wounded me.

*Perseverance* isn't a very glamorous word compared to, say, *valor* or *heroism*. But its equivalent concept, *fortitude*, has been celebrated in art, literature, and theology as one of the seven crowning Christian virtues. To muster the strength to stick with a righteous effort when you'd rather be doing something else is right up there with faith, hope, and charity.

Sometimes perseverance can even *be* heroism.

**Meditation:** Where are you challenged to persevere in righteous work this Easter season? Are you on a committee planning charitable innovation that's encountering roadblocks? Are you trying to comfort someone whose misery resists balm? Are you striving to reform some aspect of your own life? When you feel discouraged, reread the stories of the apostles' journeys and ask the Holy Spirit to deepen your commitment to perseverance.

**Prayer:** Strengthen my spirit, O Lord, when I'm tempted to take the easy way home.

## The Temptation of Pride

**Readings:** Acts 14:5-18; John 14:21-26

**Scripture:**
"Men, why are you doing this? We are of the same nature as you, human beings." (Acts 14:15)

**Reflection:** Back when I was twenty-two and a high school teacher, I took care to include contemporary, "relevant" materials in my classes. This was 1972, so among them were Bob Dylan songs, young adult novels, and movies about adolescent angst, race relations, and war. You'll never guess, though, what text my seniors liked best that year, generating the most eager discussion and the most thoughtful writing: Sophocles's classic tragedy of over-reaching pride, *Oedipus Rex*, written around 430 BCE.

Or maybe that's not such a surprise, since stories of extremely gifted, powerful humans who become blasphemously arrogant have never stopped being a staple of literary and popular narratives. From Shakespeare's Macbeth and Milton's Satan, to *Harry Potter's* Lord Voldemort and modern politicians, we're fascinated by tales of megalomaniac tragic heroes. We know they're doomed (rightly, since they disrespect "the gods" and disrupt earthly order), but we also pity and identify with their hubris. "I can see how that might happen," one of my seniors said of Oedipus. "All that praise and success has got to get to you."

What a revolutionary call to right perspective it is, then, to see Paul and Barnabas—doers of miracles and possessors of compelling eloquence—decisively resist the Lycaonians' attempt to worship them. Many with such potency would have gladly been confused with Zeus or Hermes or worshipped in their own right (like Caesars), and might even have considered such things appropriate.

"Our God is in heaven," today's psalm proclaims (115:3), dismissing false golden idols. And that's a good thing to remember at any stage of our lives—especially when the idols start to look like us.

**Meditation:** "Conductor's disease," a friend of mine terms the temptation to believe you're personally responsible for everything good that happens on your watch—a temptation that can lead to Oedipus-style pride. Take time during your own successes to acknowledge the role God's hand has played, as well as others' contributions.

**Prayer:** Create a clean heart in me, O God. Let me humbly acknowledge you as the power behind my accomplishments.

## Sharing Faith Stories

**Readings:** Acts 14:19-28; John 14:27-31a

**Scripture:**
[T]hey called the Church together. . . . Then they spent no little time with the disciples. (Acts 14:27-28)

**Reflection:** Before 9/11 tightened security protocols, it was common at the Salt Lake City airport to encounter large, organized groups of people gathered at gates. Excited and noisy, toting balloons and signs, they welcomed home returning Mormon missionaries, young people who had completed two-year proselytizing assignments in far-flung places. Getting through the crush could be annoying if you had a tight connection. Still, the affirmation of supportive community was impressive, even more striking if you knew these greetings were just the first way those missionaries would become catalysts of community-building. Soon they would report formally to their wards (parishes), vicariously involving others in their faith-promulgation adventures.

Catholic parishes don't often send out long-term missionaries these days. Nevertheless, our members do commonly venture beyond church walls in support of faith—whether far away to conferences, classes, retreats, overseas medical or social-service work, sacred sites, or locally to food banks and shelters. Unfortunately we too-often miss our chance to make these missions an opportunity for reinforcing our faith identity. We may greet such missionaries with a casual "How was it?" but rarely do we invite them to talk publicly and in depth about how their experiences touched their faith—and perhaps to help us to imagine missions of our own.

Paul and Barnabas were so much wiser when they "spent no little time" recounting at Antioch the details of their revolutionary first mission to the Gentiles. For this new community, that tale of peril and heroism, of Spirit-driven success, must have offered unimaginable validation and soaring inspiration.

We could use some of those things ourselves, in these latter days.

**Meditation:** Who in your church has recently participated in outreach, education, or community service ministry? Invite them for coffee, dinner, or a walk, and take time to learn about their experiences. If they are willing, plan an event to share that information more broadly in your Catholic community.

**Prayer:** Risen Lord, help me to overcome reticence and share my faith stories, encouraging others to spread your message to the wider world.

*May 18: Wednesday of the Fifth Week of Easter*

## Essential Pruning

**Readings:** Acts 15:1-6; John 15:1-8

**Scripture:**
"[H]e prunes so that it bears more fruit." (John 15:2)

**Reflection:** As an essayist accustomed to longer forms, I've found myself doing a great deal of "pruning" (a.k.a. strict editing for word count) while writing this devotional. Interesting but inessential ideas must disappear from such short reflections; examples must be strictly vetted, speculation abbreviated, phrasing rigorously condensed. I admit that cutting so much from drafts has hurt. Yet this rigor has been undeniably good writerly discipline, breaking bad habits and reinforcing good ones, and I hope it's made the result more user-friendly for busy readers.

Today's Gospel reminds me of something my grandmother once said about gardening that's also relevant to productive editing. "But honey, you have to prune them," she insisted when child-me responded in horror as she clipped her gorgeous locally famous rose bushes. She explained that cutting deadwood promoted new growth, that shaping bushes regulated the space between them to let sunlight in, promoting health and flowering. "Without pruning," she emphasized, "you won't have much of a rose garden." Or much of a book, either.

Jesus' words characterize God as a gardener after my grandmother's own heart. It's not just the obviously unfruitful who feel those shears; all must be shaped in the service of the larger garden's needs.

Undeniably such shaping can be painful, as when the early Christians in today's first reading felt their old ways threatened, or when we protest today as our pride or comfort is nicked by heavenly blades.

Like it or not, though, pruning is an essential part of our growth, just as it is for roses. We must trust that the rain, the sunlight, and the flowering will come in good time.

**Meditation:** Is God pruning your life in a way that seems inexplicable, even destructive? Reflect on the life stories of people who ultimately found that setbacks actually shaped them for the work God had planned for them, like Ignatius of Loyola (illness ended his military career), Frances Cabrini (denied a lifelong dream of missionary posting to Asia), or Nelson Mandela (imprisoned).

**Prayer:** All-knowing God, let me firmly trust your wisdom through the pruning seasons of my life.

*May 19: Thursday of the Fifth Week of Easter*

## Respectful Listening (and Speaking)

**Readings:** Acts 15:7-21; John 15:9-11

**Scripture:**
The whole assembly fell silent, and they listened . . . (Acts 15:12)

**Reflection:** Once upon a time, television and radio commentators reported the news. Now, many aggressively deliver opinions. Unwilling to listen, panelists shout over each other. Hosts interrupt guests and vice-versa. Everybody already possesses an unassailable point of view.

Two millennia ago the Jerusalem Council addressed flashpoint issues very differently. Playing by the rules of civil discourse established centuries earlier, speakers offered formal, reasoned speeches while the apostles and presbyters listened respectfully. Rather than pulling out emotional stops or insulting the opposite party's point of view, motives, or personal character, Peter and James argued from evidence that cut to the heart of the group's common values. Their rhetoric assumed that listeners were reasonable, virtuous people who shared a dedication to understanding and following God's ways. They aimed at forming and consolidating community, not fracturing it.

Perhaps it's too late for us as a deeply divided country to regain this sort of respectful discourse on a society-wide level. But we can all try to practice such consensus-building communication in the smaller segments of that culture we inhabit. In our families, with friends and acquaintances, with co-workers and customers, we can dedicate ourselves to hearing the other out with an open mind, and to making our own case with an aim to appealing to the other's best self, even as we display our own.

Above all, we must daily remind ourselves that bullying and outshouting are tactics grossly out of line for anyone who believes, as we purport to do, in a Father who urges us always to "remain in . . . love" (John 15:10).

**Meditation:** Invite a friend who disagrees with you to a respectful point-of-view-sharing session, no arguments allowed. Take turns explaining the basis of your convictions, asking questions but not arguing. After both of you have spoken, take time to identify shared assumptions, values, and goals. Thank each other for being open and for listening.

**Prayer:** Let me remember the apostles, Father, when I'm tempted to force my will on others. Help me to listen. Make me an instrument of consensus-building.

# Initiation and Its Responsibilities

**Readings:** Acts 15:22-31; John 15:12-17

**Scripture:**
"It was . . . I who chose you and appointed you to go and bear fruit that will remain . . ." (John 15:16)

**Reflection:** How glorious it is to become an initiate, one chosen for something long and greatly desired—admission to an ideal school, success on an occupational board exam, election to a prestigious council or club, appointment to a dream job, membership in the church. What a rush of happy validation we feel, what a sense of energy and optimism, what eagerness to embrace new responsibilities!

The Gentile Christians at Antioch would have experienced such feelings when the Jerusalem Council's letter (the fruit of the respectful exchange discussed in yesterday's reflection) arrived. They were now universally recognized as full members of the church, with no massive cultural changes or circumcision required. Paul and Barnabas had been right about their worthiness. No wonder they were "delighted with the exhortation" (Acts 15:31).

Now the work of living the faith as fully accepted participants could begin—and challenging work it would prove to be. They'd learn that bearing fruit would involve more effort than they might have imagined, that it would disturb their equilibrium as it demanded further growth, that it could be dangerous. Joyful as full inclusion into the faith was, it constituted only a starting point. Being a member is an active verb, they'd learn, not a one-time accomplishment.

And that's still a good thing for us to remember today, whenever a calling that seemed so righteously perfect at the beginning becomes difficult, whenever the "bearing fruit" doesn't quite turn out the way we expected when we were shiny new initiates.

**Meditation:** Recall a moment when you found yourself chosen for or joining something you'd deeply desired. Relive the excitement, but also remember what overly simple expectations you held. How do the demands of ongoing, active membership challenge you? If the thrill of being included in a group you currently inhabit has been blunted, resolve to bring a spirit of anticipation and adventure to today's responsibilities, as if you were a brand-new initiate.

**Prayer:** Help me to remember my initial enthusiasm, O God, as the challenges of a calling unfold before me. Keep me faithful, optimistic, eager.

*May 21: Saturday of the Fifth Week of Easter*

## Mysterious Ways

**Readings:** Acts 16:1-10; John 15:18-21

**Scripture:**
When they came to Mysia, they tried to go on into Bithynia, but the Spirit of Jesus did not allow them. (Acts 16:7)

**Reflection:** As I've mentioned before, I've consulted commentaries while preparing these reflections, and for the most part they've served me well by enriching and clarifying Scripture. Today, though, curious about why the Holy Spirit might twice have forbidden Paul, Silas, and Timothy from taking their second missionary journey to Asia Minor and instead directed them to Europe, I found the experts themselves unable to reach a decisive conclusion. Bithynia (in present-day Turkey) appears to have been no more dangerous or difficult than anywhere else, and before long Paul did in fact establish churches in that region. Why, then, did the Holy Spirit reroute them when they'd already journeyed partway to Asia?

While we may never know, commentators do agree that the apostles' cheerful acceptance of this directive provides a textbook model of obedience. Paul and his companions don't even try to reason through or contest the order. Instead, they simply, trustingly heed the dream vision's call to travel to Macedonia, accepting as the Old Testament prophet did that God's thoughts are not our thoughts, nor are our ways God's ways (cf. Isa 55:8).

Frustrating as this sentiment might be for those who like concrete answers, it's one whose truth has been oft-repeated. "God moves in a mysterious way / His wonders to perform," the eighteenth-century English poet William Cowper wrote in a particularly lyric phrasing, one whose words became text for a venerable, widely beloved hymn.

Or, as Thomas Merton wrote more recently in plainer but also beautifully balanced language, "The real hope is not in something we can do, but in God, who is making something good out of something we cannot see."

**Meditation:** If a major detour in your own plans to serve God leaves you feeling confused and struggling to impose logic on events, consider Merton's prayer from his collection *Thoughts in Solitude.* If we desire to please the Lord, it affirms, we're invited to trust that the Holy Spirit "will lead [us] by the right road, though [we] may know nothing about it."

**Prayer:** May I always follow where you lead, all-wise God, even when I do not understand the direction.

*May 22: Sixth Sunday of Easter*

## Many Gates

**Readings:** Acts 15:1-2, 22-29; Revelation 21:10-14, 22-23; John 14:23-29

**Scripture:**
It had a massive, high wall, with twelve gates where twelve angels were stationed and on which names were inscribed . . . (Rev 21:12)

**Reflection:** "How do we get into this place?" my friend asked. Travelers that morning, we were attempting to attend daily Mass at an historic cathedral in the American Southwest, but the great front doors and other portals we'd tried were locked, even as bells rang invitingly. At the last minute I peered around a corner and glimpsed a latecomer hurrying through a small, inconspicuous door. "Guess you just have to know," my friend said, shaking her head.

As impressive (and complicated of access) as that lovely church was, its splendor—and the extensive splendor of even the greatest earthly cathedrals—pales beside John's description of the "new Jerusalem" (Rev 21:2), a city whose description sounds like that of an ornate temple. A vast metropolis bright with gigantic precious stones? Jasper? Crystal? That would be something to see.

Significantly, though, the feature John spends the most time describing is the city's twelve gates. His readers, familiar with walled cities, would have known that gates were often named to imply who might use them (Jerusalem's included the sheep gate, for those bringing animals to a nearby market, and the Damascus gate on the road to and from that city). John tweaks that tradition in a marvelously inclusive way. This city's gates, he reveals, are named both for Israel's tribes and for the apostles, implying welcome not just for Jews but for all who accept the gospel transmitted through Christ's followers.

The truly glorious thing in this city, it might be argued, isn't its over-the-top magnificence, but its assurance that each faithful believer will be certain to find a personally designated gate.

**Meditation:** Identify the best, most characteristic ways you serve and love God. Then, in the joyfully inclusive spirit of today's reading from Revelation, imagine what might be inscribed on the gate of the new Jerusalem meant for your form of service. Servants of the poor? Bringers of comfort? Ministers of the word?

**Prayer:** Let me live my days in peace as I follow you, Lord, trusting that I will in time enter with great rejoicing into your magnificent dwelling.

## Sustaining Models

**Readings:** Acts 16:11-15; John 15:26–16:4a

**Scripture:**
[A] woman named Lydia, a dealer in purple cloth, . . . listened, and the Lord opened her heart to pay attention to what Paul was saying. (Acts 16:14)

**Reflection:** So, Paul and his companions heed the call and go to Macedonia, and it turns out that their first convert isn't the man in the dream (Acts 16:9) but a woman—a well-off, influential woman living on her own, a woman offering exactly the resources the mission needs to establish a foothold. This fact should cheer all who seek to acknowledge the essential role and resourcefulness of women in the church, as should recent scholarship demonstrating that Lydia was just one of many women who played crucial roles in early Christianity.

On a personal note, the story of Lydia has cheered me for two decades. Always having thought of myself as a happily self-actualized woman, I realized in shock when widowed at fifty just how deeply I'd absorbed our culture's emphasis on coupledom. Abruptly all-too-aware of stereotypes of widows and single women in general as pitiable "spare parts," I temporarily lost my sense of how I mattered, why I should go on living. Fortunately grace provided stories of single biblical women (Lydia, Judith) and more contemporary widow-saints (including medieval queens who founded abbeys and Elizabeth Seton)—women whose singleness opened new paths, allowing them to use their talents in previously unimagined, deeply important ways.

These sisters have become crucially sustaining models, my "tribe." They remind me to stop feeling sorry for myself and pay attention to God's voice, to open my heart and embrace opportunities.

Who are your models in Scripture, those individuals with whom you identify, who offer the exact wisdom you need? Whom do you have in mind when you say, "All you holy men and women, pray for us"?

**Meditation:** "There's a saint or a biblical model for everybody," a Benedictine nun I know says. An administrator with high standards might bond with St. Charles Borromeo; a loving wife and mother with Rachel; an inner-city teacher with St. John Bosco. If you haven't found your tribe, take time to explore the lives of the saints and the men and women of Scripture.

**Prayer:** Thank you, Lord, for the examples of holy men and women, my friends and guides.

## Yearning for Liberation

**Readings:** Acts 16:22-34; John 16:5-11

**Scripture:**
[T]he foundations of the jail shook; all the doors flew open
. . . (Acts 16:26)

**Reflection:** The word "miracle" has come to be used for anything wondrous or surprising—a vivid sunset, a new medical treatment, a happy coincidence. St. Thomas Aquinas, though, offers a more specific definition: miracles are things "done by divine power apart from the [natural] order generally followed in things." They're acts of God that amaze us and strengthen our faith.

While Catholics have always enjoyed miracle stories, the one chronicled in today's first reading is especially well-known. This dramatic narrative of Paul and Silas's escape from prison features in art, literature, and homiletic reference. It has also become a frequent musical subject, referenced in an African-American spiritual, a rousing Stanley Brothers' gospel song, and numerous compositions by contemporary Christian artists. There's even a Pinterest board with more than five hundred followers offering Sunday school crafts focused on "Paul and Silas in Prison"!

The appeal is easy to explain since, like so many miracle stories, this tale is an archetype, evoking the yearning for liberation that just about every human feels sooner or later. Ours may be only figurative jails like festering anger, guilt, fear, addiction, a sin we can't help repeating, a toxic relationship, prejudice. Nevertheless they can seem damning, impossible to escape.

Today's psalm echoes the solution offered to Paul and Silas: "Your right hand saves me, O Lord" (Ps 138:7). In the case of that specific prison-break, it also saved the jailer's soul.

Even though we may not find ourselves miraculously released from what entraps us, let us, too, heed stories that show that all things are possible with God and take courageous steps toward the freedom we need.

**Meditation:** What kinds of bondage have you experienced? If you found liberation, consider how God's hand fostered that freedom, and give thanks. If you're still in chains, put aside hopelessness and ask the Lord, capable of anything, to help you.

**Prayer:** Lord who freed Paul and Silas, be with me when I feel hopelessly in bondage. Give me strength, courage, and trust in your power to liberate me from whatever entrapments I face.

*May 25: Wednesday of the Sixth Week of Easter*

## Groping for God

**Readings:** Acts 17:15, 22–18:1; John 16:12-15

**Scripture:**
"He made from one the whole human race . . . and he fixed the ordered seasons and the boundaries of their regions, so that people might seek God, even perhaps grope for him . . ." (Acts 17:26-27)

**Reflection:** While many biblical verbs regarding humans' attempts to know God connote dignity ("search" and "seek," for example), I admit to a special fondness for Paul's use of "grope" during his speech in Athens. So often my own process feels more like instinctive, unsystematic "feeling my way" than like the organized, purposeful quest I know it should be. I pray to know God's will in moments of pain; I celebrate on a hike when, as the dear hymn says, "I look down from lofty mountain grandeur"; I'm jolted by a sense of holy presence during an ordinary hospice massage workday as a dementia patient turns to me and smiles.

For all its lack of dignity, "grope" does have a wonderfully significant implication. You only grope for something you're pretty sure is there—a door in the dark, a name you once knew. Paul's phrasing underlines that idea, emphasizing God's omnipresence in a world formed purposefully to inspire us to seek, sensing that "he is not far from any one of us" (Acts 17:27). We may be groping, but not blindly.

How different this is than embracing a simplistic god "made by human hands" (17:24), as Paul says of pagan sanctuaries—a divinity we could explain. Our God in contrast glows with mystery, inviting us to deepen our love and appreciation through the searching, to stretch the boundaries of what we dare to imagine.

**Meditation:** Dedicate yourself today to looking—"groping" —for signs that God is near you. Take time to notice his presence in a conversation, an observed encounter between other people, a kindness given or received, the beauty of a bird's flight, or a piece of art or music that comes fortuitously into your life. Consider keeping a daily list of such "touches" to make your "groping" more conscious and habitual.

**Prayer:** Sharpen my eyes, ears, and heart, O God, to sense your ever-present glory.

## Strengthened by the Clearness of Truth

**Readings:** Acts 1:1-11; Eph 1:17-23 or Heb 9:24-28; 10:19-23; Luke 24:46-53

**Scripture:**
[H]e was lifted up, and a cloud took him from their sight. (Acts 1:9)

**Reflection:** What a magnificent sight Jesus' ascension must have been, so rife with confirmations, promises, and implications! So magnificent, in fact, as to be overwhelming for the apostles who stand frozen and staring open mouthed into the heavens. Renaissance slang offers a wonderful word— "mooncalves"—for people so helplessly befuddled, so overmatched by their experiences.

*What just happened?* Jesus had been crucified, yes, but he'd returned and had been with them for so long—forty days— teaching and companioning. Given the human tendency to hope that good things will last forever, the apostles may well have begun to anticipate that this companionship with the risen Lord would be an ongoing and wonderful (though strange) new normal.

Suddenly, though, Christ is gone, after a speech no more dramatic than many he's made before. We'd all need angels to move us out of our shock in such circumstances, I believe!

Pope St. Leo the Great uses the apostles' befuddlement to explain why the Lord had to return to them then leave them again. God understood, Leo says, that accepting the resurrection of the body would stretch Jesus' followers' capacity for belief to its limit, so he provided clear proof-signs (those forty days of touching wounds, eating together, hearing Christ's familiar voice). The grand gesture of the ascension itself allows them actually to witness Jesus' unity with God. Once the truth sinks in, they'll never forget what they saw or promulgate it tentatively.

"Let us give thanks . . . to the Divine management," Leo urges, to the God who strengthens our faith "by the clearness of truth."

**Meditation:** Have you ever found yourself, like the apostles, frozen and incredulous at something you didn't understand but that seemed heaven-sent? Looking back, consider how that might have been exactly the experience you needed at the time—the shock necessary to move you to a new level of faith and service.

**Prayer:** When daunting, momentarily incomprehensible change shakes me, O God, help me to trust your intentions and listen for the angels' voices.

## Facing Down Fear

**Readings:** Acts 18:9-18; John 16:20-23

**Scripture:**
"Do not be afraid. Go on speaking, and do not be silent, for I am with you." (Acts 18:9)

**Reflection:** A friend who teaches children's religious education classes reports that her students are fascinated with martyrs. There seems to be something that appeals deeply to young people, especially adolescents, in the idea of so heroically taking a stand. After all, so many famous martyrs were young themselves!

We adults, though? That's another matter. We might admire those who died for the faith, but I suspect most of us would have trouble envisioning ourselves following their lead. Can you imagine how much those torments would hurt? And we have so many carefully nurtured investments in life to lose—so many projects, responsibilities, loved ones, possessions.

Paul is no longer a young man by the time he goes to Corinth (probably in his mid-forties, according to historians' estimates). Since he's been stoned and imprisoned already, persecution for the faith is obviously not a glorious youthful abstraction for him anymore. In Corinth the threat only intensifies as circumstances take a particularly ominous turn.

The Jews, Paul's own people, attempt to turn him over to the Roman authorities, one of whom washes his hands of the responsibility. The echo of what happened to Jesus is inescapable.

Yet Paul stays, strengthened by that vision and those words of the Lord: "Do not be afraid." Contemplating his story, I think with regret of the times I've turned tail at mere discouragement or bruises to my ego, and ask God to renew in me a spirit of youthful idealism. *Speak to me, too*, I pray. *Give me some share in that bravery.*

**Meditation:** Today's reading suggests that after the vision Paul took a vow to God in Corinth (ratified by growing his hair). If you're meeting uncomfortable inner resistance in a mission of your own, consider making a formal promise to God to persist for a fixed interval, listening for his guidance.

**Prayer:** Bless me with your encouragement, O God, when I grow fearful or weary in your labor.

*May 28: Saturday of the Sixth Week of Easter*

## Learning and Teaching

**Readings:** Acts 18:23-28; John 16:23b-28

**Scripture:**
"[A]sk and you will receive . . ." (John 16:24)

**Reflection:** What a contrast they were, those two students I supervised during their first semester as writing teachers! And how wrong I was about their prospects. Brilliant and widely read, Lisa spoke frequently and confidently in the group pedagogy seminar, dominating discussion. Slower on the uptake, Anna modestly absorbed information.

Yet Lisa's very gifts proved her undoing. With her own students, she was chronically impatient, even contemptuous. She wouldn't grant that she had anything to learn from her peers or mentor (me), and she stubbornly blamed her students when her own tactics failed, alienating and discouraging them. In contrast Anna's class blossomed as she patiently communicated, gauging from her students' responses how to teach, and welcoming advice when things didn't go optimally.

The bottom line is that if you're not willing to be taught, you're not likely to be much of a teacher. If you're threatened by the suggestion that you might not have all the answers, you'll always be limited in your understanding.

288   *Saturday of the Sixth Week of Easter*

Today's first reading offers an exemplar of a learner-teacher in Apollos, a man both gifted and willing to listen. An "eloquent speaker" (18:24), he was evidently well-educated, trained in classical rhetoric as well as learned in Scripture. Yet he gratefully allowed himself to be schooled by the humble tentmakers Priscilla and Aquila, bowing to their superior knowledge of Christ. In consequence he became a teacher to be reckoned with.

"Ask!" Christ urges his apostles when they're overly passive, advice that's essential for all of us with more to learn about any subject, including faith—those of us who may well find ourselves called to guide others.

**Meditation:** Where could you use some advice or deeper understanding but have failed to ask? Have you been afraid of looking dumb? Have you been stubborn in your own view of the situation even as evidence suggests that input from others would be a good idea? Calling Apollos to mind, seek out those whose knowledge can supplement yours.

**Prayer:** God of all wisdom, help me to be a willing learner, an inquirer eager for new insight.

*May 29: Seventh Sunday of Easter*

## In Every Age

**Readings:** Acts 7:55-60; Rev 22:12-14, 16-17, 20; John 17:20-26

**Scripture:**
"I am the root and offspring of David, the bright morning star." (Rev 22:16)

**Reflection:** As I'm writing these reflections, by happy chance Venus, the morning star, is especially bright. My bedroom window faces east, and since I'm a light sleeper and an early morning writer, as my own pre-dawn rising approaches, I've enjoyed catching its nightly appearance from behind a mountain ridge and watching it climb higher in the sky. I've long loved Venus's reassuring predictability, especially when, anxious in strange places, I've glimpsed this old friend: on a wilderness backpacking trip, on another continent, once from an airplane window during an especially fraught long night journey. *Be at ease*, she says. *I'm still here, and you're still home.*

If you, like me, take comfort in contemplating the orderly (to our eyes, at least) heavens, Revelation's metaphor of Christ as the ever-dependable, ever-loving "morning star" will speak with particular clarity to your heart, too. The language of today's readings evokes gloriously reassuring cosmic continuity: "I am the Alpha and the Omega, the first and the last" (Rev 22:13); and "[Y]ou loved me before the foundation of the world" (John 17:24). It suggests that if we follow this age-to-age Jesus, despite our apparent mortality, we too can count on being enfolded into a perfect, unified body that dances eternally to God's design.

What a sad contrast Stephen's persecutors offer in our first reading, with their stubbornly narrow perspective, their covered ears, their nasty but laughable attempt to take the world's course into their own divisive hands. No morning star for them; they look down for stones. Only Stephen gazes up.

It's good, I think, to keep our curtains open—and timely, as this Easter season begins its final week, to ask ourselves: *Which direction are we looking?*

**Meditation:** How long has it been since you went outdoors at night and sat in silence, watching the stars rise and move through the sky? "The heavens declare the glory of God; / the firmament proclaims the works of his hands," the psalmist wrote (19:2). Spend time letting the order and peace of the heavens quiet your soul.

**Prayer:** Ever-faithful Christ, be my lodestar. Let me always find comfort in you.

## Blowing Where It Will

**Readings:** Acts 19:1-8; John 16:29-33

**Scripture:**
And when Paul laid his hands on them, the Holy Spirit came upon them . . . (Acts 19:6)

**Reflection:** The results of googling "Holy Spirit" would be funny if they weren't such an indictment of today's self-help mentality. "How do I get the Holy Spirit?" an FAQ inquires, commodifying mystery. Those unsure of their charisms can take quizzes. Someone who fears he's "doing it wrong" asks, "Do you have to speak in tongues to have the Holy Spirit?" ("Yes!" a fundamentalist preacher unequivocally answers.)

How infinitely far all of this is from Scripture's depiction of the Spirit—a willful, multi-faceted, grace-driven force. "The wind blows where it wills, and you can hear the sound it makes, but you do not know where it comes from or where it goes; so it is with everyone who is born of the Spirit," Jesus says (John 3:8). The Spirit "came upon" the Ephesians at their baptisms, language that clearly signals which side of the exchange was calling the shots.

I've heard stories from people certain that the Holy Spirit "came upon" them in contemporary contexts, and I'll bet you have, too. They are often accounts of glorious, uncanny, holy joy, gratitude, and inspiration. The people in question deny possession of any particular spiritual credentials—sometimes quite the opposite. Yet abruptly, apparently out of nowhere, they were gripped by a sense of indwelling, an affirmation of something beyond themselves that revolutionized their faith.

We don't "get" the Holy Spirit. It's not a self-actualization tool—not something unilaterally understood and proudly mustered.

We are its dwelling place. We are its tools.

**Meditation:** In a few days, we'll sing the Pentecost Sunday Sequence, which intones "Come, O Holy Spirit, come!" Prepare for that great feast by practicing a tendency toward humble asking—toward letting the Spirit be the Spirit, toward wonder and gratitude—by reading the Sequence aloud, or singing it if you're musically inclined (try the tune of Beethoven's "Hymn to Joy"). The words to the Sequence can be found online.

**Prayer:** Help me, Holy Spirit, to relax my can-do, know-best spirit so I'm available to do your will when and how you see fit.

## The Cycles of Life

**Readings:** Zeph 3:14-18a or Rom 12:9-16; Luke 1:39-56

**Scripture:**
Rejoice in hope, endure in affliction, persevere in prayer.
(Rom 12:12)

**Reflection:** I don't know about you, but I'm always a little disoriented when the feast of the Visitation shows up amid accounts of perilous apostolic missions and mystical end-time proclamations. Abruptly we're transported back to the beginning of Christ's earthly story decades earlier, as Mary and Elizabeth meet, pregnant with Jesus and John the Baptist, respectively. The timing does fit appropriately within our yearly cycle of celebration—just under nine months, roughly, till Christmas. Still, there's something jarring about briefly inhabiting the promise of Advent as spring yields to summer.

Yet that very juxtaposition has something important to suggest to us about holy continuity in our lives. We are reminded that budding and harvesting, living and dying, are part of the same divine cycle, all aspects of God's purpose for us. At any given moment, our own trajectories are playing out in company with the different seasons of others' lives. Someone's life is always starting as another's is ending. Someone is joyful while another mourns. The overarching architecture of the dance is multi-layered, not a unified melody but an ongoing round.

Though a foolish young person might assert that the joy of beginnings is what matters most or a bitter old one despair about personal "end times," each phase in the cycle has its own work, its own worth. Rather than envying others' seasons, we'd do better to trace the ways God has been faithful through our own changes, praying always with Mary and countless others, "I am confident and unafraid" (Isa 12:2).

**Meditation:** Notice people you meet who are in different stages of their lives. Pray for them as appropriate to their needs: in thanksgiving for their joy; for comfort in their suffering; that they might find the cheerfulness, inspiration, love, gratitude, strength, or humor they need for where they are now. Ask for what you need today, too.

**Prayer:** May my soul proclaim your greatness and rejoice in you, Lord, wherever the cycle of my life finds me.

## Farewell Blessings

**Readings:** Acts 20:28-38; John 17:11b-19

**Scripture:**
"And now I command you to God and to that gracious word of his that can build you up . . ." (Acts 20:32)

**Reflection:** "When my grandmother was nearing death," a woman I know admitted, "I was crushed. I couldn't see how I could live without her." Her grandmother had always been her closest friend and mentor in practical and spiritual matters. "She was the one who encouraged me to enter that tough Master's program in biochemistry, who was my cheerleader even more than my parents. I was struggling in school at that point and worried I wouldn't have the strength to go on." Even in her last hours, though, the older woman had reached out, summoning the younger, faltering one for a blessing that rekindled confidence and inspiration. Things wouldn't always be easy, she had advised, "But don't worry. You're one of God's own, and you have important work to do. Don't ever doubt that! Make me proud!"

Today's readings chronicle two farewell blessings, one by Jesus and the other by Paul. Like my friend's grandmother, neither tries to sugarcoat the message. Each utterance is tinged with sorrow, with the sense of each speaker's own imminent end. Paul won't return to Ephesus; Jesus faces the

Garden of Gethsemane and then death. Both blessings, though, offer listeners consolation through a sense of legacy. They emphasize the rich inheritance those left behind will obtain through faithfulness, affirming them as consecrated to God's work.

As we walk our own paths generations of followers later, let us take these blessings as our own, never doubting that we, too, belong to God.

**Meditation:** Blessings don't have to be formal deathbed affairs. Encouraging words uttered in the midst of ordinary times have the power to support others' gifts, to reassure those who are weathering challenges and discouragement, and to remind people of God's faithfulness. Vow to reach out and bless someone in this informal way during each of the remaining few days of the Easter season—and perhaps beyond.

**Prayer:** Heavenly Father, help me weather the trials of my life with calm assurance, always remembering that you have blessed and consecrated me.

## Facing the Hard Truth

**Readings:** Acts 22:30, 23:6-11; John 17:20-26

**Scripture:**
[T]he commander, afraid that Paul would be torn to pieces, . . . ordered his troops to go down and rescue Paul . . . (Acts 23:10)

**Reflection:** Today's first reading presents a truly horrific scene of violence—so shocking that I've found myself attempting to "domesticate" it, bending over backwards to apply it to the calmer reality that most of us, thankfully, inhabit. One rough draft of this reflection focused on the need to respect others during disagreements; another cautioned that doctrinal differences can obscure faith's core message of love. All these efforts have ultimately struck me, though, as absurdly inappropriate attempts to disregard the hard truth about innate human savagery and sin that Luke is highlighting.

The occasion was supposed to be a pre-trial hearing, a civil fact-finding meeting among respected Jewish leaders. Instead a violent riot breaks out; civilized people become a frenzied, potentially deadly mob.

We don't really need this story, of course, to remind us of our species' savagery, often sadly associated with misguided religious fervor. The historical litany is long: cities of Albigensians and towers of New Yorkers burning; gory public martyrdoms of Protestants in seventeenth-century Europe and of Catholics in the Far East; Auschwitz; ongoing worldwide torment of the other.

To contend that such barbarity is an aberration is simply impossible. To pretend that we ourselves don't share the potential for it is dangerous.

How great is our need, then, for the very message of rebirth into love that Paul was preaching! And how liberating it is to grasp that this transformation will begin the very moment we agree to let the Holy Spirit in, the moment we acknowledge just how much we *need* the Holy Spirit.

**Meditation:** "[A]s you, Father, are in me and I in you, . . . may [they] be brought to perfection as one," Jesus prays for believers in John's Gospel (17:21, 23). What hard truths about your own capacity to do harm are preventing you from enjoying unity with Christ and others today? What specific steps can you take to sow peace in your community, workplace, and home?

**Prayer:** Replace my heart of stone with a loving heart, Holy Spirit, whenever anger threatens to overtake me.

## Feeding the Lambs

**Readings:** Acts 25:13b-21; John 21:15-19

**Scripture:**
Jesus said to him, "Feed my lambs." (John 21:15)

**Reflection:** Several years ago I attended a First Communion party for some friends' children. As we sat on the lawn, somebody asked the kiddos—both those we were celebrating and those who were older—what aspects of Catholicism they thought were most important. One naturally said communion, another reconciliation, another enthusiastically blurted, "Father, Son, and Holy Ghost!" It was a shy little girl who finally paraphrased the essence of today's Gospel: "Take good care of people."

The Easter season's readings have offered so many examples of how the earliest Christians "took good care of people," a.k.a. feeding Jesus' lambs. Jesus' followers healed the physically and mentally ill. They shared worldly goods. They invited strangers into the new covenant. Recipients of this "good care" soon became lamb-feeders themselves, as Priscilla and Aquila did by educating Apollos.

The nurturing we see in early Christianity goes beyond the human, too, of course. Those who give so much to others are constantly being sustained by the source of all strength. The Father sends the resurrected Jesus to encourage and teach them. Miracles convince them of good news and afford earthly rescue. God's voice directs them in visions. All the new Christians in Acts are thus people who take good care of others *and* lambs who themselves need feeding.

Out of the mouths of babes—though tiny, my young friend voiced the core of our faith, a message of interdependence that ought to make us at once humble and proud.

**Meditation:** As people seeking to live holy lives, it's easy to focus on the giving we do, keeping a running tally (conscious or unconscious) to reassure ourselves we're good people. Try for a few days to notice occasions where you're the lamb—the recipient of divine generosity through human agents in matters minor (a greeting that makes you feel noticed and appreciated) or major (someone doing a substantial favor).

**Prayer:** Ever-nurturing God, let me move actively in this web of giving and receiving with humility and grateful appreciation.

## Enforced Stasis

**Readings:** Acts 28:16-20, 30-31; John 21:20-25

**Scripture:**
"[I]t is on account of the hope of Israel that I wear these chains." (Acts 28:20)

**Reflection:** As I'm writing these reflections, normal routines and associations are truncated due to COVID-19, and travel is difficult. "This is the longest time in my adult life that I haven't gone anywhere!" I heard myself complain recently. "I'm going crazy!" News stories and friends' social media posts suggest that such anxious restlessness is widespread.

How accustomed to absolute freedom of movement we've become! How quick to reach for a change of scenery as a cure for tedium, a solution to a problem, a reward for work completed.

In this immediate context, Paul's equanimity under house arrest in Rome—for *two years*—seems truly incredible. Awaiting trial, he's under guard in a rented dwelling; chains are mentioned. For someone so wide-ranging, so accustomed to adventures, the sudden shrinking of his horizons must have required immense adjustment. Yet Paul's enthusiastic commitment to proclaiming the good news persists without interruption. Marooned in the heart of cosmopolitan Rome, he finds the situation's silver lining in the access it provides to sharing Christ's message with an unprecedented range of people including pagans, recent converts, Roman citizens, slaves, and visiting foreigners.

Bishop Clement of Rome (ca. 90 CE) writes that Paul's "example pointed out the reward of patient endurance." *Endurance*—how old-fashioned, even quaint, that word seems to us who take for granted the privilege of changing our scenery or circumstances at will or whim whenever we're displeased, uncomfortable, or even just bored.

Paul's story, though, reminds us that being forced to stay put—literally or figuratively—can constitute an invitation to crucial work. Approached patiently, acceptingly, with trust in divine purpose, it can even inspire us to bear new, rich fruit.

**Meditation:** Where do you still feel stuck or imprisoned as this Easter season nears its close? How might the situation be calling you to serve God in a new way or deepen a vocation? What opportunities for serving others, learning, and growing might this stillness afford?

**Prayer:** Help me to see your will in all things, O God. Teach me how to serve you in all situations.

*June 5: Pentecost Sunday*

## One in the Spirit

**Readings:** Vigil: Gen 11:1-9 or Exod 19:3-8a, 16-20b or Ezek 37:1-14 or Joel 3:1-5; Rom 8:22-27; John 7:37-39. Mass during the day: Acts 2:1-11; 1 Cor 12:3b-7, 12-13 or Rom 8:8-17; John 20:19-23 or John 14:15-16, 23b-26

**Scripture:**
I will put my spirit in you that you may live . . . (Ezek 37:14)

**Reflection:** Of the many beautiful litanies in Scripture, the recitation of the variety of peoples present as the Spirit descended at Pentecost is surely among the most moving (Acts 2:9-11). Back when I was a lector, I looked forward each year to proclaiming that joyful catalog of nations. What an incredible redemption it chronicles for peoples once scattered at Babel and now given a second chance at unity with God and each other by the Holy Spirit, who through unimaginable grace "comes to the aid of our weaknesses" (Rom 8:26).

Celebrating Pentecost at the conclusion of the Easter season makes so much wise sense. Its triumphal message epitomizes what's been proclaimed for seven weeks: all are welcome to hear and heed Christ's good news. Our celebration elegantly aligns us with the apostles at the first Pentecost, as we ourselves stand on the brink of Ordinary Time. Like them we'll face challenges in the months ahead that we can glimpse only darkly now, including overwork that may blunt our Easter spirit despite the fire we feel today, and crises that threaten to supply our own *"Now what?"* moments.

I've traded lectoring for music ministry, so I no longer get to proclaim that reading. But I do have the opportunity to see parishioners' faces as they come forward for communion. As they process, another, more contemporary litany plays in my mind: *We are elders and children; families, singles, and widows. We are conservatives and liberals in politics and faith. We are casual and formal; converts and cradle Catholics. We are people of diverse roots and ways of life.*

As we move forward from this day and from this great season, may we always remember that we as church are one in the Spirit.

**Meditation:** In the spirit of Pentecost, dedicate yourself to reaching out to others in your parish who speak a different language, whether figuratively or literally. Ask the Holy Spirit to open channels of understanding and commit yourself to discovering and celebrating what you have in common.

**Prayer:** Come, Holy Spirit, fill the hearts of your faithful, and kindle in us the fire of your love.

# References

## Introduction

Carey Landry, "Night Is Over," in *Glory and Praise: Parish Music Program* (Phoenix, AZ: North American Liturgy Resources, 1977), 164–65.

St. John Chrysostom, "Homily on Easter: The Fruits of Christ's Resurrection," in the *Patrologia Graeca*, ed. Jacques Paul Migne, vol. 50 (Paris: 1857–1866), 439.

## May 4: Wednesday of the Third Week of Easter

John Milton, "Lycidas," in *Complete Poems and Major Prose*, ed. Merritt Y. Hughes (New York: Odyssey Press, 1957), 125.

## May 6: Friday of the Third Week of Easter

Pope Francis, "'Rigid but Honest': Morning Meditation in the Chapel of Domus Sanctae Marthae," *The Holy See* (Francis: Daily Meditations, May 5, 2017), http://www.vatican.va/content/francesco/en/cotidie/2017/documents/papa-francesco-cotidie_20170505_rigid-but-honest.html.

## May 9: Monday of the Fourth Week of Easter

John Oxenham, "In Christ There Is No East or West" (1908).

## May 14: Saint Matthias, Apostle

Peter Scholtes, "We Are One in the Spirit" (1966).

### May 21: Saturday of the Fifth Week of Easter

William Cowper, "Light Shining Out of Darkness," in *The Complete Poetical Works of William Cowper* (London: Oxford University Press, 1913), 455.

Thomas Merton, *The Hidden Ground of Love: Letters* (New York: Farrar, Straus & Giroux, 1985), 297.

Thomas Merton, *Thoughts in Solitude* (1958; New York: Farrar, Straus & Giroux, 1999), 79.

### May 24: Tuesday of the Sixth Week of Easter

St. Thomas Aquinas, "On Miracles," in *Summa Contra Gentiles: Book 3: Providence, Part II*, trans. Vernon J. Bourke (Notre Dame, IN: University of Notre Dame Press, 1975), 81–83.

### May 25: Wednesday of the Sixth Week of Easter

Carl Boberg, "How Great Thou Art," trans. Stuart K. Hine, in *Glory and Praise* (Phoenix, AZ: North American Liturgy Resources, 1987), 97–98.

### May 26: The Ascension of the Lord

St. Leo the Great, "Sermon 73: On the Lord's Ascension," in *Nicene and Post-Nicene Fathers: Second Series*, vol. 12, ed. Philip Schaff and Henry Wallace (1895; New York: Cosimo Classics, 2007), 186–87.

### June 4: Saturday of the Seventh Week of Easter

Clement of Rome, "First Epistle to the Corinthians," in *The Ante-Nicene Fathers*, vol. 9, trans. John Keith, ed. Allan Menzies (New York: Charles Scribner's Sons, 1903), 229–48.

# SEASONAL REFLECTIONS NOW AVAILABLE IN ENGLISH AND SPANISH

## LENT / CUARESMA

**Not By Bread Alone: Daily Reflections for Lent 2022**
*Amy Ekeh and Thomas D. Stegman, SJ*

**No sólo de pan: Reflexiones diarias para Cuaresma 2022**
*Amy Ekeh and Thomas D. Stegman, SJ;
translated by Luis Baudry-Simón*

## EASTER / PASCUA

**Rejoice and Be Glad:
Daily Reflections for Easter to Pentecost 2022**
*Susan H. Swetnam*

**Alégrense y regocíjense:
Reflexiones diarias de Pascua a Pentecostés 2022**
*Susan H. Swetnam; translated by Luis Baudry-Simón*

## ADVENT / ADVIENTO

**Waiting in Joyful Hope:
Daily Reflections for Advent and Christmas 2022–2023**
*Mary DeTurris Poust*

**Esperando con alegre esperanza:
Reflexiones diarias para Adviento y Navidad 2022–2023**
*Mary DeTurris Poust; translated by Luis Baudry-Simón*

Standard, large-print, and eBook editions available. Call 800-858-5450 or visit www.litpress.org for more information and special bulk pricing discounts.

Ediciones estándar, de letra grande y de libro electrónico disponibles. Llame al 800-858-5450 o visite www.litpress.org para obtener más información y descuentos especiales de precios al por mayor.